THE SUBJUNCTIVE IN ENGLISH

Alabama Linguistic & Philological Series #15

THE SUBJUNCTIVE
IN ENGLISH

by Wayne Harsh

UNIVERSITY OF ALABAMA PRESS

University, Alabama

FOR

WILLIAM VAN O'CONNOR
January 10, 1915–September 27, 1966

Chairman, Colleague, Friend

Acknowledgements

I am greatly indebted to Professor David W. Reed, without whose continuing assistance and encouragement over a period of several years I could not have completed this book. His help has been invaluable: he helped define the topic, he suggested a general *modus procedendi,* he gave me the benefit of detailed and helpful criticisms at every stage of both the research and the writing. I am also grateful to Professors Arthur E. Hutson and Madison S. Beeler, both of whom have given freely of their time and have been of much help to me in many ways.

I am also deeply indebted to Dr. R. W. Zandvoort, of the University of Groningen, for the many insights into language and language study that I gained during a year of intensive work under his direction. I am grateful to the Fulbright Commission and the United States Educational Foundation in the Netherlands for making it possible for me to study under Professor Zandvoort.

Finally, thanks are due Mrs. Marian Koritz and Mr. David M. Andersen for their assistance in verifying bibliographic information.

Wayne Harsh

University of California, Davis
February 8, 1967

Contents

Introduction

IN 1926, THE LEXICOGRAPHER HENry Watson Fowler "wrote off" the English subjunctive in an *ex cathedra* statement that Sir Ernest Gowers chose to leave intact in his 1965 revision of Fowler's *A Dictionary of Modern English Usage:*

> About the [inflected] subjunctive, . . . the important general facts are: (1) that it is moribund except in a few easily specified uses; (2) that, owing to the capricious influence of the much analysed classical moods upon the less studied native, it probably never would have been possible to draw up a satisfactory table of the English subjunctive uses; (3) that assuredly no one will ever find it either possible or worth while to do so now that the subjunctive is dying; . . .[1]

Since 1926, however, more than thirty scholars have considered it worth their time to write on the English subjunctive and its use.[2] Moreover, inflected subjunctive forms are by no means hard to find in current American usage—even in the daily newspaper. Thus, in a paper selected at random—the *Columbus Dispatch* (Columbus, Ohio) for Sunday, April 26, 1964—a number of these forms are to be found quite readily. On page 1, for example: "Did Ike Suggest to Scranton that He Not *Rule* Himself Out of Race?" [emphasis supplied]. Again, on page 26A: "The consensus is that even if he *were* at all responsible for the murder, Oswald could not have been the sole culprit" [emphasis supplied]. And again, on page 38: "There was also the rumor that though one's sins *be* as scarlet, money could buy one a grave next to the High Altar" [emphasis supplied]. It would seem, on the basis of such examples, that the inflected subjunctive, though hardly in a state of robust good health, has been taking a long time to die. But that it is dying still, as Fowler noted, can hardly be denied.

The purpose of this book is to sketch the historical pattern of the English subjunctive by means of an analysis, largely statistical, of some forty-four texts, representing English usage in a number of times and places, thereby illustrating two parallel trends: (1) a decline in the use of inflected subjunctive forms, and (2) an increasing use of a variety of grammatical structures in place of such forms.

DEFINITIONS OF TERMS[3]

Mood. This term refers to verbal inflections or to syntactic contrasts that (1) denote by formal opposition the relations between one verb in the sentence and another verb structure, and (2) express a notional contrast that supposedly indicates the attitude of the speaker or writer toward the action or state of affairs expressed by the verb. Traditionally, English is said to utilize three mood categories, depending on whether the speaker or writer considers a syntactic structure as stating a fact (indicative mood), as a command (imperative mood), or as expressing non-fact or modification of fact (subjunctive mood).

The subjunctive mood, generally referred to in this book as the "subjunctive", is formal opposition shown by verb inflection *or* syntactic contrast indicating (1) the relationship(s) between one verb in the sentence and another verb structure expressing wish, command, desire, etc., and (2) that the speaker or writer is thinking in terms of non-fact or modification of fact, as distinct from fact (indicative mood) or command (imperative mood). In present-day English such inflectional contrasts usually occur only in the third person singular present tense of the verb (e.g., *play/plays*). The single exception to this rule is the anomalous verb *be;* in addition to the usual contrast *be/is,* contrasts also occur in the present tense first and second person singular and in all persons plural (e.g., *be/am; be/are*), and in the preterite first and third person singular (e.g., *were/was*). Hence,

Indicative: He says he *feels* bad.
Subjunctive: Lodge suggested that White *show* it in strict confidence to Balfour, Clemenceau, and Nitti.
Indicative: If the subject of the first member *is* a personal pronoun, it is repeated.
Subjunctive: If it *be* asked what the subjunctive in the above sentences expresses, the answer is threefold.
[Emphasis supplied in all sentences.]

Structures of modality, i.e., constructions expressing modality that are frequently used in syntactic structures in which inflected subjunctives formerly occurred, are for present purposes: (1) modal auxiliary constructions and (2) modal preterite inflections.

"Modal auxiliary constructions" are verbal structures in which one of the auxiliary verbs (e.g., *may, shall, will*) is used along with a main verb to express a modal relationship similar to that described above as "subjunctive". Such constructions have been classified according to a substitution pattern outlined by Poutsma[4] that restricts modal classification to those periphrastic constructions for which it is possible to substitute an inflected subjunctive form. For example:

> *Modal auxiliary construction:* I will pray that your brother's life *may be spared.*[5]   [Emphasis supplied.]
> *Inflected-subjunctive equivalent:* I will pray that your brother's life *be spared.*   [Emphasis supplied.]
> [Diachronic considerations relative to such patterns of substitution are discussed under the heading Classification of Modal Preterite Inflections, in Appendix A.]

"Modal preterite inflections" are verbal structures in which a preterite inflection is used not to express contrast between present and past time but to indicate a subjunctival modal relationship. For example:[6]

> *Modal Contrast:* It's high time somebody *held* his tongue.
> *No Modal Contrast:* When I *have asked* a London policeman the way, I *have* invariably received a polite answer.
> *N.B.* The term *modal,* as used in the definitions above, is restricted to the meaning conveyed by the phrases "modal auxiliary construction" and "modal preterite inflection", and is not to be confused with the non-restrictive term *modal,* which is sometimes used indis-

criminately in reference to auxiliaries in general or to grammatical structures that express modality. (See Appendix A.)

In the investigation of subjunctive patterns, only the written language was used. Therefore, non-graphic or suprasegmental indications of mood (discussed by Wilde [*Aufforderung, Wunsch und Möglichkeit*] and Kruisinga [*A Handbook of Present-Day English*]⁷) are not considered.

PATTERNS INVESTIGATED

The specific developments and patterns discussed in this book are as follows:

1. The historical pattern of declining use of the inflected subjunctive, with particular attention to
    (a) varying patterns of decline in the different semantic–syntactic categories (wish, command, conditional clauses, etc.), and
    (b) varying patterns in dialectal usage in the Middle English period and in present-day British and American English.
2. Significant patterns in non-subjunctive grammatical structures used to express non-fact or modification of fact (referred to in this book as "structures of modality" and designated "modal auxiliary constructions" and "modal preterite inflections"), with particular emphasis on
    (a) historical patterns of usage according to type of structure, and
    (b) patterns of usage according to syntactic category.
3. Significant patterns, found in present-day English trans-

lations, of non-modal grammatical forms and constructions (infinitives, participles, etc.) that are used in
syntactic structures markedly similar to those in which
a subjunctive or structure of modality was habitually
used in earlier English. In addition, note has been
made of the appearance of indicative or "common
mood" verb forms and imperative mood forms in syntactic constructions in which a subjunctive or structure
of modality was formerly used.

Chapter One

Studies of the English Subjunctive

IF A CURSORY EXAMINATION OF recent linguistic studies tends to contradict the dogmatic opinion expressed by Fowler concerning the uselessness, if not the impossibility, of delineating the English subjunctive, a closer examination of descriptions of the subjunctive offered in the past half century tends to substantiate A. G. Kennedy's observation, in 1935, that "there has always been more uncertainty among scholars regarding the nature and definition of [grammatical] mood than about any other of the so-called [verb] properties".[1]

Later authors have reaffirmed the trend toward uncertainty. Thus, three of the more recent publications range from an emotional—and, one must note sadly, an inaccurate—argument in favor of putting a stop to what the writer sees as an "unexpected revival" of the subjunctive,[2] through another less emotional, but questionably documented, argument in favor of acknowledging that an English subjunctive certainly does exist,[3] to an article accusing several scholarly writers (among them the grammarians Albert H. Marckwardt and Arthur G. Brodeur) of using the hyper-correction *were* for *was* after an introductory *if*.[4] Such scholarly free-for-all, and the "woolly thinking" displayed in a specific article on the subjunctive that had appeared in a prominent American journal, led the Dutch grammarian R. W. Zandvoort in 1963 to term the " 'Subjunctive' one of the most confused and confusing chapters of English grammar".[5]

The very category "mood", with its semantic implications and psychological connotations, has been a stumbling block for notionalists and formalists alike. Grammarians who have avoided the temptation of defining it wholly in psychological terms (e.g., seeing the subjunctive as expressing "images of the twilight world of imagination", or as evidence of national or racial characteristics[6]) have not been able to exclude mental concepts completely from their descriptions of mood. J. R. Kantor, in a psychologically oriented discussion of the subject (*An Objective Psychology of Grammar*, 1952), accurately criticizes the descriptions of mood offered by the disciples of grammatical meaning (Sonnenschein), and grammatical form (Jespersen), and by adherents of purpose criteria, whom Kantor labels "traditional grammarians". Kantor concludes: "We may infer that moods are stylistic matters organized by the grammarian on the basis of a knowledge of the choice and use of words in formal discourse". (The grammarians G. O. Curme and R. W. Zandvoort, among others, had previously pointed out the stylistic function of mood.[7]) More usefully, Kantor writes

When we regard moods as varying psychological types of linguistic adjustments, we cannot escape the question whether linguistic patterns are in fact limited in number. There is a tremendously large range of linguistic situations and we have not found in grammars any good criterion for fixating [sic] a definite number of forms for an exclusive mood designation.[8]

As a solution to the problem of mood classification (or at least description), Kantor proposes the study of speech patterns as forms of "psychological adjustment". Such an approach might well prove to be worthwhile someday, but until the disciplines of linguistics and psychology can offer a much more complete classification of language patterns than is now available, continuing reliance must surely be placed on the methods and findings of more traditional linguistic research.

In considering the English subjunctive, such findings may properly be restricted almost entirely to those of modern descriptive grammarians, since earlier treatments of grammatical mood were marred by a tendency to impose some preconceived classical pattern on English, or are so notional in description as to be of little value. As Britta Marian Charleston writes in her *Studies on the Syntax of the English Verb*

When dealing with the problem of the moods in English grammar, the grammarians [of the seventeenth and eighteenth centuries] were confused by the example of Latin grammar with its modal endings. Thus some (such as Cooper, Maittaire, Ward) adopt the Latin moods and give their English equivalents (usually by means of auxiliary verbs) ; others (such as Greenwood and Loughton) consider that English grammar has no moods (or at the outside one, the indicative, since there are no modal endings), but they also give the English equivalents of the Latin moods; others again (especially White) take as a starting-point the theoretical functions of mood and explain how these may be expressed in English. On the whole, the treatment of moods by these grammarians of the 17th and 18th century shows a confusion and hesitancy which is still to be observed today. . . .[9]

The tenor of the arguments in the early nineteenth century is illustrated by the following passage from Goold Brown's *The Grammar of English Grammars* (1862) :

The *subjunctive* mood is so called because it is always *subjoined* to an other [sic] verb. It usually denotes some doubtful contingency, or some supposition contrary to fact. The manner of its dependence is commonly denoted by one of the following conjunctions; *if, that, though, lest, unless.* The indicative and potential moods, in all their tenses, may be used in the same dependent manner, to express any positive or potential condition; but this seems not to be a sufficient reason for considering them as parts of the subjunctive mood. In short, the idea of a "subjunctive mood in the indicative form," (which is adopted by Chandler, Frazee, Fisk, S. S. Greene, Comly, Ingersoll, R. C. Smith, Sanborn, Mack, Butler, Hart, Weld, Pinneo and others) is utterly inconsistent with any just notion of what a mood is; and the suggestion, which we frequently meet with, that the regular indicative or potential mood may be *thrown into the subjunctive* [sic] by merely prefixing a conjunction, is something worse than nonsense.[10]

And early in the twentieth century traditional grammarians were still dogmatically pronouncing a "notional" view of the subjunctive. Thus, in 1904, C. T. Onion told readers of his *Advanced English Syntax:*

> It is incorrect to say (as is sometimes said) that the Subjunctive, except in the case of *be* and *were,* is an extinct Mood. It is true that these are the only distinctively Subjunctive forms in common colloquial use; but we have seen already in dealing with the Cases, that where there has been an extensive decay of inflexions, it is necessary to consider *meaning* rather than *form;* and this principle must be applied here also.[11]

Late in the nineteenth century, however, certain historical or "descriptive" grammarians had already begun to approach the problem of the subjunctive in a rather different manner. In their works an attempt was being made, for the first time, to describe the subjunctive scientifically, in terms of objective, verifiable linguistic data. Two of these early scholars, Jespersen and Poutsma, documented and described the modal patterns of English rather fully, and analysis of the current status of the English subjunctive may properly begin with their findings.

The formidable work of Otto Jespersen is an especially advantageous starting point, since his grammatical point-of-view, as expressed in *The Philosophy of Grammar* (1924), may be characterized as "moderate", as compared to the views of both his more traditional and his more revolutionary contemporaries.

Classifying mood as a syntactic rather than notional category, Jespersen summarily dismissed the traditional idea—still popular in the 1920's—of categories of meaning. However, he emphasized the fact that the subjunctive as a form is difficult to characterize, trace, or compare:

The truth seems to be that the subjunctive was at first
vaguely used in a variety of cases which it is impossible
logically or notionally to delimitate as against the use
of the indicative, and that each language took its own
course in sometimes restricting and sometimes extend-
ing its sphere of employment, especially in dependent
clauses. The vagueness of the meaning of the subjunctive
facilitates the transition of a present subjunctive to a
future indicative as in the Latin forms in *–am,* and the
extension of the second person singular in the strong
verbs from the subjunctive to the indicative, e.g. OE
wære. In many cases the levelling of the two moods may
have been brought about by formal coalescence, but even
apart from that there is in many languages a strong
tendency to get rid of the subjunctive. In Danish and
Russian there are only a few isolated survivals; in English
the subjunctive has since Old English times been on
retreat, though from the middle of the nineteenth century
there has been a literary revival of some of its uses.[12]

A further indication of Jespersen's medial position is
the diachronic description of the subjunctive pattern in
Modern and present-day English that is to be found in
the later volumes of his monumental *A Modern English
Grammar.* This description—though scattered through the
book under such headings as "Imaginative use of Tenses",
"The Auxiliary", "Personal Endings in Verbs", and
"Mood", and unfortunately never coordinated or summarized—helps to complete his account of the decline of
the subjunctive from its important status as a paradig-
matic modal form in Old English to its minor role in
present-day English. Though he listed the constructions
that are currently used in syntactical structures in which
the subjunctive formerly appeared, Jespersen left to other

grammarians the task of classifying and interpreting these new inflections and constructions.[13]

Poutsma, in an early and systematic description of the subjunctive (*A Grammar of Late Modern English*, 1926), completed part of the task of classifying and describing the new constructions, which he termed "substitutes". Stating that

> . . . ordinary language has almost entirely discarded mood-inflection and even, to a large extent, its periphrastic substitute, in all cases where they are not needed, substituting for them the indicative, or rather the neutral mood.

Poutsma's book provides a detailed synchronic analysis of the subjunctive pattern, with numerous diachronic reflections, and a discussion—under the modal categories of "Subjunctive" and "Conditional"—of the auxiliaries *(may, might, shall, should, will, would)* used in forming the "periphrastic subjunctive" and the tense forms (preterite) used in forming the conditional mood.[14]

Two later studies exemplify the tendency of descriptive grammarians to observe a strictly formal definition of mood and to trace more-or-less actual patterns of subjunctive usage—in contrast to the approach of grammarians who insist on a notional definition of mood and who propose hypothetical subjunctive paradigms. The earlier, more traditional study is that of Curme (*A Grammar of the English Language*, 1931), in which the author states his "philosophy" of the subjunctive as follows:

> To the conservative grammarian all change is decay. . . .
> He is fond of mourning over the loss of the subjunctive and the present slovenly use of the indicative. He hasn't

the slightest insight into the fine constructive work of the
last centuries in rebuilding the subjunctive.

With this philosophy in mind, Curme describes the
change of the subjunctive to a system of periphrastic
modal forms with the inflected subjunctive retained only
in "literary style" and traditional expressions. He defends
at length the advantages of this change:

> As the simple subjunctive forms in the course of a long
> phonetic development lost their distinctive endings, modal
> auxiliaries were pressed into service to express the same
> ideas. In large measure they are subjunctive forms, al-
> though not recognizable by a distinctive ending. . . . The
> endings of the old simple subjunctive were doubtless more
> concrete than they were even in the oldest English. They
> had become mere abstract symbols, so that even in the
> Old English period the English mind was already seeking
> a more concrete and a more accurate expression for its
> subjunctive ideas, and began to employ the auxiliaries
> which are now so much used. The fact that some of these
> auxiliaries were employed at a time when the subjunctive
> had distinctive endings shows clearly that they did not
> come into use on account of the lack of distinctive sub-
> junctive forms. The use of the auxiliaries evidently in-
> dicates a desire for a more concrete and a more accurate
> expression of thought and feeling. The auxiliaries have
> more and brighter shades of meaning than the old simple
> subjunctive forms.[15]

More original by far is the treatment of the subjunctive
in C. C. Fries' *American English Grammar* (1940). Interestingly, this study, which is part of a report on research
in informal correspondence conducted with the techniques
of structural linguistics (considering exclusively the forms
of words and word order), reveals the same facts as do

more traditional investigations. Fries' summary of his findings affirms the basic conclusions of traditional grammarians:

> (1) In general the subjunctive has tended to disappear from use. This statement does not mean that the ideas formerly expressed by the inflectionally distinct forms of the verb called the subjunctive are not now expressed but rather that these ideas are now expressed chiefly by other means, especially by function words. . . . (3) The failure to use the subjunctive form in non-fact conditions, and in "that" clauses after words of asking, requesting, suggesting, etc., is not a characteristic of Vulgar English only. The practices of Standard English and Vulgar English do not differ significantly in this respect.[16]

As might well be expected, not all recent investigations and interpretations of the subjunctive pattern complement each other so neatly as the four just described. Many scholars have skirmished on both sides of the middle ground held by Jespersen. On the one hand, a few staunch traditionalists have clung to the idea of an inflected subjunctive paradigm, albeit one that, as a practical matter, now differs very little from the indicative.[17] Opposing them diametrically are grammarians such as Kruisinga, who in his *An English Grammar* (1941) recognizes a modal preterite and an *irrealis* but insists that

> The use of the stem in the above cases would not justify us to speak of the existence of a subjunctive in English. By a subjunctive we understand a system of verbal forms existing by the side of another system (the indicative) and used to express a variety of modal relations which it is not necessary to specify for our purpose. Needless to say, English does not possess such a system, in contrast, for instance, to French and German.[18]

Five very recent studies of present-day English verb inflections confirm Kruisinga's assertion that current English has no subjunctive paradigm. However, all of them do consider the few remaining subjunctive forms, and two of them include discussions of structures that are now commonly used in place of subjunctive constructions.

Bernard Bloch, in a discussion of "English Verb Inflection",[19] states that the verb *be* is unique in having optative and concessive uses *(God be praised; The public be damned)* and in a footnote remarks

> The optative use of *be* is paralleled by other verbs in a few formulas: *God have mercy; God forbid; Perish the thought.* The concessive use of other verbs than *be* is limited to such archaic locutions as *Try they never so hard.*

Bloch notes the use of *be* as a finite present ". . . only after *if* and only in rather formal style *(If I be not mistaken; If you be he; If they be still here . . .)* ". Bloch also notes the existence of a non-preterite form *were* and adds a new category to cover its patterns:

> Complementary distribution and identity of meaning have allowed us to treat the two preterit forms *was* and *were* as both containing the zero alternant of suffix 2. But there is another form *were* which is not preterit and which contrasts with *was:* the form that appears in conditional clauses after *if* with a subject in the 1st or 3d person singular *(If I were rude, I'd apologize; If he were here, he'd see it;* contrast *If I was rude, I apologize; If he was here, he saw it.).* This *were* must be an inflected form different from the preterit *were;* its category we may call (with Hockett) the UNREAL. Again we analyze the form *ad hoc:* base alternate /wəh/, suffix morpheme /r/.

However, Bloch does not consider the non-preterite use

of verbs in such modal preterite constructions as "It's high time somebody *held* his tongue", or "I wish I *was* wonderful", both of them constructions commonly used in present-day English.[20]

Professor W. F. Twaddell, in his study *The English Verb Auxiliaries* (rev. ed. 1963) notes the use of the so-called "past" form to signal a focus on non-reality in conditional clauses, and of *would*, both as a polite form and a form used to signal "lesser assurance in predication". Twaddell labels as relics such present-day English constructions as: "I insisted that he be here at five" (base form of the verb preceded by "that" + subject in indirect discourse imperatives [*ask, suggest, demand*, etc.]). However, the statistics reported in this book indicate that this construction exhibits one of the few subjunctives still frequently used—though of course it may, as Professor Twaddell suggests, soon give way to *catenatives* ("oughtn't to") and to modals with prescriptive or contingent components ("should[n't]", "must[n't]").[21]

Two recent descriptions of the subjunctive in present-day English, those of R. W. Zandvoort and James H. Sledd,[22] were drawn upon for definitions and terminology used in this study (see Appendix A). Since both descriptions are given in handbooks, rather than in detailed studies of verbal structures or of English accidence and syntax, these treatments of the subjunctive are brief and restricted. Professor Sledd, discussing the term only in a glossary notation on "Subjunctive Mood", gives a straightforward, traditional definition, omitting all comment on historical developments and patterns of usage. More valuable for purposes of the present research is his definition of "Modal Auxiliary", in which he points out the use of a verbal structure expressing modality to indicate the relation of one verb (*verbal* according to Sledd's terminology) in the sentence to another, as in the example sentence he uses, *I suggest that the window should be closed,* in which Sledd states ". . . the auxiliary *should* is used in a nominal clause, the object of *suggest*".[23]

Professor Zandvoort, though also brief in his treatment of "Mood and Modality", gives a workable formal definition of the subjunctive and points out the restricted usage of subjunctives in present-day English. Basing his definition of the subjunctive on the formal oppositions used in a language, Zandvoort writes

> The pair *play—plays* has been shown to represent the opposition between the third person singular present tense on the one hand, and the other persons of the singular plus those of the plural on the other. In literary English, however, it also represents an opposition on a different plane: the third person singular of a verb may occur either with or without *s;* the form without *s* is known as the *subjunctive,* the one with *s* as the *indicative,* and the difference is said to be one of mood.

He further defines mood as

> . . . a verbal category represented in English by the opposition *(he) play—(he) plays,* of which the former (subjunctive) denotes non-fact, the latter (indicative) either fact or non-fact.
> The difference between the subjunctive and the indicative denoting non-fact is one of style.

Zandvoort is equally clear and concise in his discussion of modal preterite inflections:

> Of far greater importance for the structure of present-day English is the opposition *play(s)—played* in the function described in 139 and 140 [sections discussing the

modal preterite]. As there explained, the function of the preterite in the sub-clauses of sentences expressing something desirable or conceivable, or denoting a wish or a condition not likely to be fulfilled, is not to express a contrast between present and past time, but between reality and desirability or (im)possibility (the so-called *modal preterite*). In the cases of 219 *(I wish it were over . . . If I were you, I should go . . .)* it coincides with the opposition subjunctive—indicative. . . .[24]

In an article published more recently than the above statements ("On the So-Called Subjunctive", *English Language Teaching,* Volume XVII, January, 1963, pp. 73–77), Professor Zandvoort makes the interesting suggestion that the term *subjunctive* be dropped: "The term has done too much harm; and for a description of the linguistic phenomenon indicated, it is not really required" [p. 77]. In the article, Zandvoort summarizes the still pervasive influences of the traditional grammarian's notional definition of the subjunctive and goes on to propose the following description of *s*–less verb forms:

"A verb is a word that takes an *s*–suffix when serving as a non-past, non-optative predicate to a subject in the third person singular"—does not sound too bad as a working definition, and probably takes care of ninety-nine per cent of the cases that one is likely to come across in living English.

The last two of the five very recent statements on English verb inflection are particularly interesting for their authors' attempts to deal with the semantic or psycholinguistic aspects of modal usage. Both deal with such implications, however, on a far more objective plane than does Kantor. Frank Behre, in his *Notes on Indicative Clauses of Condition,*[25] discusses the use of mood in literature and in logic, suggesting that numerous non-linguistic elements help determine the choice of mood:

> My choice of modal expression, then, is determined, to a great extent, by the resistance I anticipate in the mind of the hearer. But at the same time I have regard for the needs of meeting the resistance in my own mind. To say about a notorious liar "if he is honest" would normally be as irritating to my own sensibility as I expect it to be to the sensibility of the hearer; and to say "if he were honest" about a person whose honesty I have not the least reason to doubt would hardly satisfy me even if I took a very pessimistic view of human nature."

Behre suggests further that the percentage of modal use is determined by the type of material (e.g., poetry compared with criticism). The interesting and well-argued thesis of Behre's monograph is that rhetorical purpose, at least in earlier English, sanctioned the use of the conditional clause of condition *in indicative mood* used in context as part of a "proposition" for the sake of argument and demonstration. (Behre had suggested earlier [*Meditative–Polemic SHOULD in Modern English THAT–Clauses*] that differentiation in modals reflects the speaker's attitude and, at times, the speaker's desire to impose a certain idea.)

Professor Martin Joos, in *The English Verb: Form and Meanings* (1964), gives a description of the meanings conveyed by English modal auxiliaries or "markers" *(will, shall, can, may, must, ought to, dare, need)* that is well documented, explicit as to semantic implications of the respective markers, and convincing in both argument and illustration. Joos classifies the markers as follows:

> Casual modals (WILL, SHALL, CAN, MAY) *take* that relation from the *minimal* social matrix of events,

where the determining factors are the resultant of chance and whim operating upon the items that populate the factual world of accepted reality; but the

Stable modals (MUST, OUGHT TO, DARE, NEED) *find* that relation in the *maximal* social matrix of events, where the determining factors are eternal and omnipresent: they are the community mores. Accordingly, stable modals exclude remote tense.

Adequate modals (WILL, CAN, MUST, DARE) derive their force from *completeness* in the set of determining factors; but the

Contingent modals (SHALL, MAY, OUGHT TO, NEED) get their weakness from some *deficiency* in the determining factors.

Assurance (WILL, SHALL, MUST, OUGHT TO) comes from *penalties* for failure of the specified event to occur; but

Potentiality (CAN, MAY, DARE, NEED) comes from *immunity* in case the actor brings the event to completion.[26]

Using a set of symbols to indicate syntactic, semantic, and psycholinguistic definitions and restrictions applicable to the modal markers, Joos discusses the modal functions (according to the various categories listed), using as textual evidence the reported conversation at an English murder trial and the reporter's comments. In addition to providing a rather complete description of the modal auxiliaries, his study indicates that many more kinds of data (including the use of intonational patterns in indicating meaning) can be observed and analyzed than linguists have utilized to date. Joos also disposes of the still more-or-less standard notion that such modals as *will* denote futurity:

At this point it's about time to dispose of the notion that

will is a "future tense" auxiliary. Like *every* modal, and simply because "time will tell" whether the asserted relation of the specified event to the real world suffices to bring about its occurrence, it has a *connotation* of futurity; but *no* modal has a denotation of futurity.[27]

Joos' documented illustrations support his point quite adequately.

STUDIES OF THE SUBJUNCTIVE IN THE VARIOUS HISTORICAL PERIODS

In addition to general descriptions of the English subjunctive contained in monographs, histories, grammars, and handbooks, a number of specific studies of the subjunctive (individual texts and according to particular syntactical categories) in the Old and Middle English periods are cited elsewhere in this book, but two particularly thorough and detailed works should be considered here.

The earlier of the two, Frank Behre's *The Subjunctive in Old English Poetry* (1934), is valuable both for its treatment of the stated topic and for its lucid and comprehensive discussion of grammatical forms and syntax in relation to the subjunctive. Though Behre limited himself to the Old English period, the book includes a brief general history of the subjunctive that helps to explain in part the long-existing confusion of terminology in modal descriptions. "The Old English subjunctive," Behre states,

> is an inheritance from Primitive Germanic. The Germanic subjunctive, in its turn, combines in itself the functions of two Indo–European modal form–groups, *viz.* the

modus conjunctivus and the modus optativus, which were preserved as formally distinct categories in Aryan languages and Greek. Concerning the fundamental functions of these two moods there has been, and is, considerable diversity of opinion among writers on mood–syntax. The most current view is that of B. Delbrück, whose account of the functions of the conjunctivus and the optativus may, with slight modifications, be summarized thus: The *modus conjunctivus* was used to express 1) wish, precept, and concession, 2) conditionality (covering the two aspects 'potentiality' and 'unreality') . . . .

The Germanic subjunctive corresponds, on the formal side, chiefly or exclusively, to the IE. optativus. With regard to its functional character, it has features characteristic of both the IE. moods outlined above. Hence, from a comparative point of view, the Germanic subjunctive is to be regarded as a survival of the IE. optativus, which has also taken over at least some of the meanings of the IE. conjunctivus, which modal form group has become obsolete in Germanic languages.[28]

The second specialized study, Hans-Oskar Wilde's "Aufforderung, Wunsch und Möglichkeit", published in *Anglia* in 1939–40, comprises two book-length articles on developments in the subjunctive from Old through Modern English *(Neuenglisch)*. Wilde imputes questionable sociological, political, and psychological significance to the linguistic data, and sees the subjunctive as a key to understanding the foundations of the British way of life:

> Das Willensproblem ist ein Grundthema englishcher geistiger Auseinandersetzung. Die Frage des guten Willens ist die Frage des Gentleman–Ideals.

Nevertheless, this work provides a good deal of useful information on patterns of the English subjunctive, especially on such matters as the early development of the modal auxiliary construction and its usage in later historical periods; the relation of subjunctive forms (or structures of modality) to verbs in syntactically related clauses; and the usage patterns of modal constructions in prose and poetry. In treating the Renaissance period, which he reports separately from the *neuenglischen* period, Wilde uses a variety of literary types (prose, poetry, dramatic texts) ; in the *neuenglischen* portion of the study he restricts his textual analysis to prose works. The research data reported in the study are of great value. Almost as uniformly, however, the author's non-linguistic interpretations are largely worthless—a fact well-illustrated by his concluding sentence:

> Die Schlüsselstellung des Konjunktivs für grundsätzliche Erörterungen und für den Versuch einer Deutung des Wesens, der Geschichte und der Lebendigkeit des englischen Gemeinwesens wurde sichtbar.[29]

In sum, twentieth-century grammatical studies generally confirm a subjunctive pattern similar to that outlined by Jespersen. Whereas English formerly had a fully inflected subjunctive with a usage pattern similar to that of Latin or Modern German, its present-day verb system allows relatively few formal distinctions of mood. Except for (1) a very few stereotyped expressions, (2) the incidental employment of the subjunctive in dependent noun clauses, and (3) occasional contrasts in word order that indicate subjunctive mood or, in the second person, verb forms that indicate imperative mood, the distinctions of mood that are still expressed in English are denoted by periphrastic forms (using the modal auxiliary constructions) or by preterite tense forms (referred to in this study as "modal preterite inflections"). Certainly, as Fowler observed, no subjunctive paradigm can properly be said to exist in present-day English.

Chapter Two

Biblical Translations

SIX TRANSLATIONS OF THE NEW Testament, ranging in date from *ca.* 800 to 1923, are compared in this chapter.* As regulated by a count of finite-verb structures in the Rushworth Gloss, the textual sampling was restricted to Chapters 7–14 of *The Gospel According to St. Matthew,* in each version of which (a) approximately 1,000 finite-verb forms were analyzed, and (b) subjunctive forms and structures of modality were designated as to type and classified as to syntactic category.

*In chronological order, the following:
1. Latin text, *ca.* 800: *The Rushworth Gospels* [completed *ca.* 800]

2. Old English, *ca.* 950: *The Rushworth Gospels* [English gloss, completed *ca.* 950]

For purposes of comparison, non-subjunctive forms and constructions (i.e., infinitives, participles, or verbs in the indicative or imperative mood) that were used in some of the texts in structures in which a subjunctive appeared in one or more of the other translations were classified and tabulated.

In addition to the general secondary sources that were used in determining criteria of modal designation (see Appendix A), a number of more specialized references were utilized.[1] As related to the six texts, the criteria taken from these special secondary sources were as follows:

1. *Rushworth Latin Text:* In designating subjunctives and classifying them as to syntactic category in the Latin text, the grammar *Latin Fundamentals* (3rd ed., 1958), by E. L. Hettich and A. G. C. Maitland, was consulted. One category, the causal subjunctive (e.g., *quia non egreserent poenitentiam*, Matt. 11:20), was not included in the data, since the structure is peculiar to Latin and invariably shows an indicative form in English.[2]

2. *Rushworth Gloss:* Sampling in the Rushworth Gloss was restricted to the manuscript that is now known as Rushworth₁, and which is in the hand of one glossator, Farman or Faerman.[3] Inflected endings for the subjunctive, in addition to the regular *-e, -en* forms, include for the present *-ae, -e, -a, -an,* and *-on,* and, for the preterite, the plural endings *-an* and *-on* plus frequent *-n-*less plurals

---

3. Middle English, ca. 1389: *The Gospel of Matheu, Mark, Luke, and Joon in Englische* [Wycliffe translation, completed ca. 1380]

4. Modern English, 1526: *The Gospell of S. Mathew, S. Marke, S. Luke, and S. Ihon* [Tyndale translation]

5. Modern English, 1611: *The Holy Bible* [Authorized King James Version]

6. Present-day English, 1923: *The New Testament, An American Translation* [Goodspeed translation]

(Sievers) .[4] In addition, the uninflected infinitive in Rushworth₁ shows, besides the regular ending *–an,* the endings *–en, –on, –un,* and shortened forms in *–e, –a,* and *–æ,* a fact that is sometimes pertinent to verbal analysis in this study. Since the normal ending for the present indicative plural was *–aþ,* the forms in *–en* and *–on* were considered distinctive subjunctive forms if tense and mood could be established by syntactic analysis. In designating preterite plural forms it was necessary to use syntactic comparison for classification, and *–an* and *–on* forms were classified as non-distinctive subjunctive forms. If confirmed by syntactic study, forms ending in *–æ, –e,* and *–a* in the singular and *–n*-less plurals ending in *–e* were classified as subjunctives since they present a formal contrast to the regular indicative endings of *–est, –eþ, –aþ* and *–on.*

3. *Wycliffe Translation:* The dialect of this late Middle English text was established by Skeat as definitely Midland, and possibly of Oxford in the Southwest Midlands.[5] The central dialects during this period, according to Reed, showed both *–n* and *–n*-less forms in the present indicative as well as the subjunctive (as contrasted with *–th* indicative verb endings in the Southern dialect and the *–s* indicative endings in the Northern dialect). Hence, in designating many of the present plural subjunctive forms in the text it was necessary to use a pattern of syntactic comparison, with the result that a large number of these forms were classified as non-distinctive subjunctives. In addition, as Ortmann pointed out (*Formen und Syntax des Verbs bei Wycliffe und Purvey,* 1902), Wycliffe frequently shows an "inorganic" *–e* in such strong verbs as *cam(e)* and *ȝaf(e).*[6] Therefore, preterite singular forms of such verbs were analyzed by syntactic comparison with unambiguous subjunctive structures in order to determine

whether the form should be classified as a non-distinctive subjunctive or excluded as an atypical indicative form.

Among the 1,000 (+) finite verb forms and structures examined, in each version a total of 133 were found to involve either a subjunctive or a structure of modality in at least one translation. Designation as to modal type and classification as to syntactic category of the 133 forms are reported in the tables and figures [given on page 148ff].

Table 1, in addition to showing verb totals, indicates the total number of subjunctive modal structures for the respective versions, with sub-totals according to modal type and according to syntactic category of the subjunctive structures. The graph in Figure 1 illustrates both the over-all decline in the use of all types of subjunctive structures (with a sub-peak of usage in the King James version) and the contrasting rise and later decline in the use of modal auxiliary constructions and modal preterite inflections. The percentages for subjunctives and structures of modality are shown in Table 2, as are percentages of modal structures per total finite verbs. Figure 2 indicates in percentages the greatly varying incidence of non-distinctive forms. Figure 3 illustrates patterns of usage according to syntactic category.

The types and incidence of non-subjunctive grammatical constructions appearing in certain translations, in alternation with subjunctives or structures of modality in at least one other translation, are shown in Table 3. The totals indicate the number of non-subjunctive structures used, the types of grammatical form or construction, and the syntactic categories of the subjunctive structures found in one or more of the translations.

The most obvious and significant pattern discernible

in the biblical statistics (which are displayed in Tables 1, 2, and 3, and Figures 1, 2, and 3) is an almost uninterrupted decline in the incidence of the inflected subjunctive. Almost equally significant, if not so marked, is a decline in *all* types of subjunctive modal structures, as evidenced by the mere sixteen subjunctive modal forms in the present-day American version, compared to sixty-five such constructions in the Old English version. Even taking into account the fact that the earlier version is a gloss and, as such, was undoubtedly much influenced by its Latin model (despite the originality of the glossator, as discussed below), the percentage of decline in forms indicating modality seems extremely high. A third pattern, probably more interesting as a stylistic influence than as a linguistic development, is the relatively high incidence of subjunctive modal forms in the King James version.

The patterns of usage of the two different types of structures of modality (given in percentages in Table 2), while showing a constant tendency to encroach into what might be termed "subjunctive territory", reveal several interesting variations. The modal auxiliary constructions show the greatest increase, going from 6 per cent in the Old English translation to 62.5 per cent in the American version. Almost reaching their peak in greatest number of occurrences with twenty-four structures in the Wycliffe version, they give way slightly to modal preterite inflections in the Tyndale version (seventeen modal auxiliary constructions against twenty-two modal preterite inflections), then reach a peak of twenty-six occurrences in the King James translation. The modal preterite inflections build more gradually to a peak (twenty-two occurrences, constituting 41.5 per cent of all subjunctive structures) in the Tyndale translation. The percentage of usage drops to 21.4 per cent in the King James version, then rises to show a sub-peak of 37.5 per cent in the American translation.

Non-distinctive subjunctive modal structures in a percentage table computed in ratio with distinctive forms show, as might be expected, a distinct peak in the Middle English translation by Wycliffe (with twenty-two occurrences, representing 39 per cent of the total of distinctive and non-distinctive subjunctive modal structures) and sub-peaks of 17.7 per cent and 15.8 per cent, respectively, in the Old English and present-day English translations (see Table 2 and Figure 2). This high percentage of non-distinctive subjunctive forms in the Wycliffe version accounts for the lower incidence of distinctive subjunctive modal forms in the Wycliffe translation than in the later Tyndale version (see Figure 1). If non-distinctive structures were tabulated with subjunctive modal structures (as they are in the sub-totals of the columns in Table 1), the pattern of decline of total subjunctive modal forms would indicate a gradual decline until the King James version. It should also be noted that the high percentage of non-distinctive forms in the American translation is attributable to (a) the relatively small number of modal constructions and (b) the fact that certain modal auxiliary constructions are grammatically ambiguous.

The totals of non-subjunctive forms and constructions used in syntactic structures in which at least one of the translations uses a subjunctive modal form (Table 3) show a somewhat peculiar pattern, maintaining plateaus in the Old English and Wycliffe versions (each of which has fifty-four such structures) and in the Tyndale and King James versions (seventy-seven and seventy-four structures, respectively), and occurring most frequently in

the American translation, with its one hundred and four-
teen structures. The sub-totals according to the grammatical type of the alternating structures reveal a prepond-
erance of indicative mood verbs in each of the translations,
and an increasing use of infinitive constructions in the
later ones, particularly those of Tyndale and Goodspeed.
The sub-totals within the grammatical types, which show
usage according to syntactic category, indicate (a) a consistently high incidence of indicative mood forms in time-
category structures, (b) the frequent use in present-day
English of indicative forms in conditional structures, and
(c) frequent use in present-day English of infinitive constructions in purpose clauses.

Patterns of usage according to the syntactic category of
the subjunctive or structure of modality (see Table 1 and
Figure 3) reveal continuing usage in certain categories,
namely: Indirect Narrative, Purpose, Conditional, and
Relative Clauses. The most frequent are conditional structures which, from the Middle English period to the present day, consistently show the highest total incidence, and
which account for ten of the sixteen subjunctive modal
forms to be found in the American translation. Several
categories—Command, Noun Clauses, and Time—continue
to use subjunctive structures through Modern English.
Non-subjunctive forms and constructions exhibit the patterns relative to syntactic category that are mentioned
above, and which are indicated by the second sub-totals
in Table 3.

In interpreting the patterns of usage disclosed by all of
these data, it is necessary to consider certain factors, linguistic and otherwise, that influenced the translations in
general, the individual translations, or both.

It is almost beyond dispute, for example, that the most

decisive influence on at least the four earliest of the English translations examined was the very nature of scriptural prose, with its formalized and often archaic diction and syntax.

Account must also be taken of the fact that *all* of the biblical texts—unlike most of the other texts considered in this book—*are* translations. But it is quite evident, on the basis of the data shown in Table 1, that the early translators were not slavish imitators; there were distinct differences between Latin and English usage, particularly in such syntactical categories as Time, Condition, and Relative Clause. Working against this impulse to originality, however, was a tendency of successive English translators (up to and including those who did the King James version) to pattern much of their work on preceding translations. This fact, often noted by historians of scriptural translation, is illustrated and confirmed by the durability of such formulaic expressions as the purpose clause, "That it might be fulfilled", or the phrasing of the Lord's Prayer—the latter a formulaic passage that shows subjunctive forms even in the Goodspeed translation.

In addition to these rather paradoxical general influences, which affected all five English translations in greater or lesser degree, each translation was subject to certain influences peculiar to it alone.

1. *Rushworth Gloss.* As Skeat has noted, the glossator generally followed the Lindisfarne Gloss very closely and in glossing St. Mark even copied Latin word order; but he was surprisingly original in his handling of *The Gospel According to St. Matthew.* The result, in Skeat's opinion, was an essentially new version, something more in the nature of a translation than a mere linear gloss.[7]

2. *Wycliffe Translation.* Also based on a Latin version,

this translation often follows Latin verb structures more closely than does the Rushworth Gloss, particularly in such features as the use of participial constructions for narrating action. Compare, for example: *"at ille respondens . . ."* (Rushworth Latin text) and *"And he, answerynge . . ."* (Wycliffe) [Matt. 12:48]. In terms of the total number of finite verbs used, the Wycliffe translation is the closest to Latin of the five English translations (see Table 1), but in subjunctive usage patterns it compares closely with the other English versions.

3. *King James Version.* The noticeable sub-peak in subjunctive usage in this translation (illustrated in Figure 1) is quite readily explained with but a minimum of research into the history of biblical translation. The Very Reverend Hugh Pope, discussing the prescribed use of certain preceding translations (the Bishop's Bible, 1568) and the preferred use of the Genevan and Rhemish versions, provides details concerning earlier versions that the King James translators utilized, and cites Henry Hallam's criticism of the style and language of the King James version, as follows:

> . . . but one remark as to a matter of fact cannot reasonably be censured, that in consequence of the principle of adherence to the original versions which had been kept up ever since the reign of Henry VIII, it is not the language of the reign of James I. It may, in the eyes of many, be a better English, but it is not the English of Daniel, Raleigh, or Bacon, as any one may easily perceive. It abounds, in fact, especially in the Old Testament, with obsolete phraseology, and with single words long since abandoned, or retained only in provincial use.[8]

More detailed (and more enlightening) are the remarks of J. M. Grainger, appearing in a syntactical study in which he proposes that the King James version recorded past syntactical developments in a way that summed up the transition from Late Middle to Early Modern English.[9] In Grainger's view, the translators, while necessarily following contemporary usage to some extent, also took past usage into account. Grainger's remarks on the subjunctive, while perhaps questionable as to stylistic hypotheses, are otherwise factually accurate and informative. He writes

> The Bible, while showing a marked preference for the old direct subjunctive forms on account, no doubt, of their brevity, archaic dignity, and more popular sound, nevertheless admitted the newer periphrastic forms in practically all constructions requiring subjunctive. . . . [Such tendencies] did much to preserve the old as well as to propagate the new forms. . . .

Noting that "the tendency to substitute the indicative outright for the subjunctive appears just incipient in the King James Version", Grainger lists the example "If any may *be* a worshipper of God and *doeth* his will, him he heareth" (John 9:31), and remarks

> The commonest verbs, such as *be, go,* and *do,* use the subjunctive almost invariably, though even with them an indicative form is sometimes seen masquerading where a subjunctive would be expected and might seem more regular.

4. *American Translation.* The deliberate avoidance of archaic language or formalized grammatical structures in Goodspeed's translation of the New Testament was noted by the translator in the preface to his 1923 edition:

> The New Testament was written not in classical Greek, nor in the "biblical" Greek of the Greek version of the

Old Testament, nor even in the literary Greek of its own day, but in the common language of everyday life. This fact has been fully established by the Greek papyrus discoveries and the grammatical researches of the last twenty-five years. It follows that the most appropriate English form for the New Testament is the simple, straightforward English of everyday expression. . . . The aim of the present translation has been to present the meaning of the different books as faithfully as possible, without bias or prejudice, in English of the same kind as the Greek of the original. . . .[10]

The result of Goodspeed's effort to avoid either an "elaborate, elegant style" or a conscious "literary style" is a translation that stands in almost direct contrast to the deliberate archaism and formal, literary style of the King James version.

Illustrative of the linguistic features affecting the pattern of subjunctive usage in the respective texts are the specific examples of the modal structures that were used, and particularly the atypical structures, alternating structures, or structures ambiguous as to designation and classification. Subjunctives and structures of modality used regularly in the translations are indicated by designation of the structure and passage in the King James version as listed in Appendix B. Some representative examples of atypical structures, alternation in structures, and ambiguous structures are given below:

1. *Atypical Structures: Zero–Verb Forms.* One of the most interesting structures of modality is what might be called a zero–verb subjunctive. Such structures, though technically not subjunctives, illustrate the arguments of Kruisinga and Wilde (among others) for consideration of suprasegmental indicators of mood.[11] Two such verb-

less structures occur in the text investigated. The first, indicated in tabulation since one version uses a verb, is as follows for the six versions:

Rushworth Latin: *ue tibi chorozain ue tibi beth-saida* . . .   [changed construction, zero–verb form]
Rushworth Gloss: *wa þe chorazam & wa þe beth-saidæ* . . .   [changed construction, zero–verb form]
Wycliffe: *Woo to thee! Corozaym, woo to thee! Beth-saida* . . .   [changed construction, zero–verb form]
Tyndale: *Wo be to the! Chorasin, wo be to the! Betzai-da* . . .   [subjunctive]
King James: *Woe unto thee, Chorazin! woe unto thee, Bethsaida* . . . [changed construction, zero–verb form]
Goodspeed: *Alas for you, Chorazin! Alas for you, Bethsai-da!* . . .   [changed construction, zero–verb form]
(Matt. 11:21)

The second structure, not tabulated in this study since it shows no finite verb in any translation, is in Matt. 10:12 of the Wycliffe version: ". . . *sayinge Pees to this hous*". It is translated in King James as an imperative clause: ". . . *salute it*".

2. *Alternation in Structures within a Text.* The Rush-worth Gloss in particular shows variation in use of the subjunctive (see also below under "Alternation in structures between the texts"), often using subjunctive and indicative interchangeably in translating similar syntactical structures as in the conditional structures in Matt. 7:9 and 7:10, which are respectively in text and gloss:

Text: *si petierit filius suus panem . . . aut si piscem petierit* . . .
Gloss: *þe hine bidde sunu his hlaf . . . oþþe gif he fiscæs biddeth* [sic] . . .

In these instances, the Rushworth$_1$ glossator has translat-

ed the Latin conditional structure first as a relative clause
and then as a conditional clause using indicative mood.
In the result clause of Matt. 13:54, the variation of indicative–subjunctive seems even more arbitrary, when the
scribe glosses the passage as follows:

> Text: *docebat eos . . . ita ut mirarentur et dicerent*
> Gloss: *gelærde hiæ . . . swa þaet hiæ wundradun &*
> *cweden . . .*

Other translations also show variation in the types of
modal structures used, the Wycliffe version of Matt. 7:9
and 7:10 showing respectively the following subjunctive
and modal auxiliary constructions:

> *ȝif his sone axe breed . . . Other ȝif he shal axe a fishe . . .*

In translating structures that are similar but require
different tense forms in the auxiliaries, the translators of
the Old and Middle English periods show confusion, translating two slightly differing relative clauses as follows:

> *ait illi tu es qui venturus es . . .*   [participle]
>
> *cwæþ to heom fereþ secgaþ arþu seþe cwome scalt . . .*
>   [modal auxiliary construction]
>
> *Seide to hym, Art thou he that art to cummynge . . .*
> (Matt. 11:3)   [indicative mood]
>
> *ipse est helias qui uenturus est . . .*   [participle]
>
> *he is se elias seþe cume* scal . . .* [**cuome,* alt. to *cume*]
>   [modal auxiliary construction]
>
> *he is Ely that is to cume . . .*   [indicative mood]
> (Matt. 11:14)

3. *Alternation in Structures between the Texts.* A good
deal more diversity is, of course, shown in the construc-

tions used in the different texts in translating identical structures and in verb forms used in syntactic structures that are identical or nearly so. Certain patterns have already been noted—as, for instance, the almost consistent use in the English texts of non-subjunctive forms in expressing clauses dealing with time. Uniformly, the English versions show only indicative mood verbs (or, very rarely, participles) in structures in which the Latin *cum*–circumstantial with subjunctive mood verb is used. However, when the clause shows a temporal relationship and also denotes expectancy or anticipation (Latin *donec*), it also includes a subjunctive form in some versions. Examples of the two types, both classed under Category 10: Time, are as follows:

Rushworth Latin: . . . *cum autem introisset* . . .

[subjunctive]

Rushworth Gloss: *þa he þa eode* . . .   [indicative mood]

Wycliffe: *Sothely when he hadde entride* . . .

[indicative mood]

Tyndale: *When Jesus was entered in to* . . .

[indicative mood]

King James: *And when Jesus was entered* . . .

[indicative mood]

Goodspeed: *When he got back to* . . .
(Matt. 8:5)   [indicative mood]

Rushworth Latin: . . . *donec eiciat ad victoriam iudicium*

[subjunctive]

Rushworth Gloss: . . . *oþ þæt ut asendeþ to sigor in dome*

[indicative mood]

Wycliffe: . . . *til that he cast out dome to victorie*
                                    [non-distinctive subjunctive]

Tyndale: . . . *tyll he sende forth judgement unto victory*
                                                    [subjunctive]

King James: . . . *till he send forth judgement unto victory*
                                                    [subjunctive]

Goodspeed: . . . *until he carries his judgement to success*
(Matt. 12:20)   [indicative mood]

In Rushworth$_1$ there is considerable variation in conditional structures, both variation within text and in comparison with the Latin and the other English versions. Contrary to the pattern described by Quirk and Wrenn,[12] the glossator sometimes used the subjunctive when the terms of the situation seemed quite possible, e.g., Matt. 8:31: *"gif ðu ut awearpa usic"*, for which all other translators used an indicative or common mood form. (However, the modern and present-day English versions show non-distinctive forms that have not been considered subjunctives in this study.) In contrast, the Rushworth Gloss has an indicative form (as do the Latin and the American versions) in the quite similar clause from Matt. 12:11: *". . . & gif fealleþ þæt in seaþ . . ."* [*þæt* referring to a sheep], whereas the three other English versions have a subjunctive form. Again, in stating what seem to be impossible conditions, the Rushworth glossator used an indicative mood verb in Matt. 12:26: *"gif þonne wiðerweard se wiþerwearð ut-weorpeþ . . ."*, in contrast to the subjunctive forms used in the Tyndale and King James versions.

In the three conditional structures cited above, the Rushworth Gloss and the Latin text agree. In other conditional structures, however, the gloss (but not the Latin) shows subjunctive forms, as in Matt. 10:13:

> *et si quidem fuerit domus digna veniet pax vestra super*
> *eam . . .*
> *gif þæt siæ hus wyrþe cyme sibb eowra on . . .*

—a structure in which only the Latin and present-day American translations do not use a subjunctive in the protasis. However, the Lindisfarne Latin text, which (in Skeat's opinion) the Rushworth glossator probably consulted, does show a subjunctive form *(veniat),* classified as command type, in the apodosis.

Quite frequently, as shown in the statistics of Table 1, the Rushworth Gloss is similarly unique in having a subjunctive in a relative clause structure, as in the formulaic expression, *"seþe haebbe earan gehernisse, gehere"* (Matt. 11:15), and again in *"seþe gemoete, saule ł ferh his forlease þæt"*, though in the latter clause in the sentence the Rushworth Gloss also shows an indicative structure: *". . . & seþe forleoseþ ferh his for mec he gemoeteþ þæt"* (Matt. 10:39).

Only in the King James version is a subjunctive used to express command in the formulaic expression: "Son, be of good cheer; thy sins *be* forgiven thee" (Matt. 9:2, 9:5). This structure was designated subjunctive by syntactical comparison with unambiguous subjunctives of the Command type in the King James version (as in Matt. 8:13: ". . . so *be* it done unto thee"). Also, in the portion of the King James version considered here, the verb *be* in the third person is used only for the purpose of showing subjunctive mood contrast.

4. *Use of Structures of Modality in the Translations.* The early use of modal auxiliary constructions is illustrat-

ed above (*sepe cwome scalt; sepe cume scal*) in the Rushworth Gloss of Matt. 11:3 and 11:14. The use of a modal
auxiliary construction in Wycliffe was also shown in the
conditional structures of Matt. 7:10: "Other ʒif he *shal axe*
a fishe, wher he *shal dresse* to hym a serpent". A much
more interesting early use of modal preterite constructions is illustrated in Matt. 12:11, which appears in the
Tyndale version as: ". . . iff he had a shepe . . .", in contrast to the Wycliffe: ". . . that hath oo sheep . . ." and the
King James: ". . . that shall have one sheep . . . ." What appears to be a modal preterite construction even as early as
the Rushworth Gloss is shown in Matt. 11:21, in which the
conditional structure is translated as follows in the Rushworth₁, Wycliffe, and Tyndale versions:

> Rushworth Gloss: *forþon þe þær in tyro & sidone
> geworht werun maegen þe worht werun in eow Iara in
> wite & ascan hreuwnisse dydun*
> Wycliffe: *for ʒif the vertues that ben don in you hadden
> ben don in Tyre and Sydon . . . thei hadden done
> penaunce . . .*
> Tyndale: *for if the miracles which were showed in you
> had been done in Tyre and Sidon, they had repent-
> ed . . .*

5. *Ambiguous Structures.* Structures that are ambiguous
in designation are relatively infrequent in the biblical
texts under analysis, perhaps in large measure because a
number of versions were available for comparison, and
the Latin text could be used as a referent. The designation of the *þæt*–clause in Matt. 8:4, Rushworth Gloss:
"& *cweþ to him haelend gesech þæt þu naengum sæcge*",
presents a problem more orthographical than syntactical in
nature, since Quirk and Wrenn list the spelling *secge* as
subjunctive and the spelling *sæge* as imperative.[13] The

syntactic structure of the clause is rather similar to indirect commands such as the one in Matt. 9:30: "... *cwæþ ende geseaeþ þæt þis nænigmon wite*", except for the fact that the clause subject of the former structure is in the second person singular. For present purposes, since the verb form could be interpreted as either an imperative or a subjunctive, it was designated as Category 3: Indirect Narrative, non-distinctive. (The Latin version of the structure in question shows an indicative future tense form, whereas the other English translations show imperatives [e.g., "See thou tell no man"].)

Two other structures were ambiguous as to designation in the later English versions, since the modal auxiliary constructions that were used do not allow an unambiguous pattern of substitution. The conditional structures of Matt. 9:21 in both apodosis and protasis were difficult to classify. The inflected form in the protasis of both Rushworth$_1$ and Wycliffe is non-distinctive, and the Latin, following the usual pattern for expressing quite possible conditions, uses an indicative form. Structures used in the three later English versions are as follows:

Tyndale: *Yff I maye toche . . . I shall be safe*
King James: *If I may but touch . . . I shall be whole*
Goodspeed: *If I can just touch his cloak, I will get well*

Since the substitution pattern, *If I* [he] *touch his cloak, I* [he] *get well*, gives a slightly different meaning to the expression, the structure was classified as non-distinctive for all forms except the indicative form in the apodosis of Rushworth$_1$ (. . . *hal ic eam ł beom*) and the Latin text showing indicative forms in both clauses.

In the indirect question construction of Matt, 10:19, though the Rushworth$_1$ form is subjunctive (Sievers, see page 37 and Note 4), the Wycliffe form is non-distinctive, and the modal auxiliary constructions of the Tyndale and King James versions are ambiguous in a pattern of substitution and are therefore designated as non-distinctive. The forms for the five English versions are the following:

> Rushworth Gloss: *ne þencaþ ge hu oþþe hwæt ge sprece . . .*
> Wycliffe: *nyl ʒe thenke how or what thing ʒee speeken . . .*
> Tyndale: *take no thought howe or what ye shal speake . . .*
> King James: *take no thought how or what ye shall speak . . .*
> Goodspeed: *have no anxiety about how to speak or what to say . . .*   [infinitive construction]

In summary, the biblical translations, which cover a chronological period of roughly a thousand years, illustrate the following patterns of subjunctive usage:

1. The pattern of usage of subjunctive modal structures shows a rapid and continuous decline, from which the only deviation is a slight increase in the King James version. The seeming increase of modal structures, beginning as early as the Tyndale translation, may be accounted for by the high percentage of non-distinctive subjunctive forms in Wycliffe's Middle English translation. Inflected subjunctive forms in the material investigated decline to non-existence in the Goodspeed translation.

2. Structures of modality in the Old, Middle, and Modern English translations show patterns of increase that are almost inverse to the pattern of decline of the inflected subjunctive. Modal auxiliary constructions reach a peak in numerical frequency of usage in the King James version and a peak in percentage of usage per total of modal structures in the present-day English translation. Modal preterite inflections reach a peak both in numerical fre-

quency and percentage of usage in the Tyndale version, with a sub-peak in percentage of usage in the present-day English version. Like the inflected subjunctive, both types of modal structures show a marked decline in total number of occurrences in the present-day English version.

3. Non-distinctive subjunctive forms show a peak in both numerical frequency and percentage of usage in the Middle English (Wycliffe) translation, and sub-peaks in percentage of usage in the Old English and present-day translations. The high percentage of non-distinctive forms in the Goodspeed translation is attributable to the fact that it includes relatively few structures of modality and to the grammatical ambiguity of certain modal auxiliary constructions.

4. Non-subjunctive forms commonly used in alternation with a subjunctive modal structure in at least one of the other translations are, according to frequency of occurrence, as follows: indicative mood forms, infinitive constructions, imperative mood forms. Significant patterns in alternation of subjunctive–non-subjunctive structures according to syntactic category of the subjunctive are as follows: Time–category subjunctives alternate most frequently with indicative mood forms; Purpose–category subjunctives alternate most frequently with infinitive constructions; Result–category subjunctives alternate most frequently with indicative mood forms.

5. Certain external influences include the deliberately archaic nature of the King James version and the contrasting, deliberately simple, idiomatic, and non-literary nature of the present-day English translation.

6. The most marked features of linguistic influences as shown by textual evidence are (a) the alternation of subjunctive–non-subjunctive structures in identical or similar

syntactic structures within and between the texts, and (b) the early use and rapid development of modal auxiliary constructions and modal preterite inflections with the modal auxiliary constructions frequently showing modal ambiguity in the present-day English version.

Chapter Three

Secular Texts and Translations in Old and Middle English

COMPARED TO PRESENT-DAY BIB-
lical translations, the translations into modern usage of
certain early English secular writings do not exhibit so
pronounced a decline in the use of the subjunctive. However, they do show a pattern of subjunctive usage that
contrasts significantly with that of the original texts.*

The translations of the *Chronicle*[1] and *The Tale of
Melibee*[2] have only one-third as many inflected subjunctives as the originals (65 to 20 and 33 to 11, respectively) —
declines of upwards of 200 per cent. However, the number
of subjunctive modal structures in the texts and transla-

*The texts compared in this chapter are the following:
1. *ca.* 1121, 1122 *Peterborough Chronicle* (MS Bodley Laud 636,
first hand) [*ca.* 1121, 1122]

tions differs far less sharply (see Table 4), and it is the patterns of usage according to modal type indicated by these data that seem rather significant. As shown in Table 5 and in Figure 4, the totals of subjunctives and modal auxiliaries in text and translation form nearly symmetrical patterns of chiasma; that is, the translations have approximately the same percentages of modal auxiliary forms per total modal structures as the originals have of inflected subjunctive forms, and vice versa. (An exception to this generalization is to be noted in the case of *The Parson's Tale* and its translation.)

The use of modal preterite inflections shows a chronological pattern quite similar to that of the biblical analysis, with a high percentage in use in the Middle English texts and a high positive correlation between original texts and translations (see percentages of usage in Table 5). The percentage of non-distinctive subjunctive forms per

-----

2. 1953 *The Anglo–Saxon Chronicle* (E), as translated by G. N. Garmonsway [1953]

3. *ca.* 1387–1392 *The Tale of Melibee* and *The Parson's Tale* (*The Canterbury Tales*) [*ca.* 1387–1392]

4. 1934 *The Tale of Melibeus* and *The Parson's Tale,* as translated by J. U. Nicolson [1931]

Textual sampling in the *Chronicle* covered entries for the years from 656 to 1001 inclusive. Approximately fifteen hundred finite verbs (regulated according to count in the original text) were analyzed, and a total of one hundred seventeen verbs were designated as showing a subjunctive or structure of modality in the original, the translation, or both. Textual sampling in *The Canterbury Tales* was restricted to the first 500–plus finite verbs in the tales themselves (the prologues were excluded from the investigation). In the textual material required to furnish five hundred non-subjunctive finite verbs, the total number of verbal constructions showing subjunctive modality in either the text or translation were seventy-seven in *The Tale of Melibee,* thirty-nine in *The Parson's Tale.*

total subjunctive structures that is shown for the original texts also compares with the percentages of non-distinctive forms shown in biblical translations of the Old and Middle English periods. That is, all three secular texts show a relatively high percentage of non-distinctive subjunctives, with a peak in the Middle English period. However, unlike present-day English biblical translations, as exemplified in that by Goodspeed, two of the translations of the secular texts show no non-distinctive forms, and the third has a very low proportion (5.5 per cent) of such forms.

With respect to use of non-subjunctive constructions in either original text or translation in alternation with a subjunctive in translation or original, there are many in the translations of the *Chronicle* and *Melibee* (see Table 6), but relatively few in the uniformly conservative translation of *The Parson's Tale*. The sub-totals in Table 6 reveal that indicative mood forms are most frequently used in contrast with subjunctive structures, and that infinitive constructions are the next most frequent substitutes. The figures on alternation of non-subjunctive forms according to syntactic category reveal frequent use of indicative forms in translations, as compared with subjunctive structures used in indirect narration and in noun clauses in the original texts, and, in the *Chronicle*, frequent use of infinitive constructions in the translation in place of subjunctives expressing indirect narration in the original (e.g., *bed him þet he scolde him giuen . . . asked him to give him . . .* [963]). A high sub-total of changed-form constructions in concessive clauses is shown in the translation of *Melibee* because of the change of the conjunction-verb-pronoun construction *al be it* to the subordinating conjunction *although* (e.g., *al be it so that she*

perilously be wounded; although she is perilously wounded
[line 1014]).

Statistics on the use of subjunctive modal constructions according to syntactic category reveal a usage pattern in the translations that is almost identical with usage in the original texts, with exceptions to be noted only in categories of result and relative clauses in the translation of *The Parson's Tale.* This pattern of continuing usage in all categories, which contrasts sharply with the pattern in biblical translations, is largely attributable to the conservative nature of the secular translations.

In interpreting the evidence concerning secular writings it is difficult to ascertain or to assess the various influences that make for unique patterns of subjunctive usage in the three texts and their translations, particularly since these influences often fall within the realm of stylistics. The *Chronicle* is hard to classify as to genre, since it can hardly be classed as literature, and yet it is, at times, something more than a mere diary or historical chronicle. The specialized nature of the textual material—a recording of natural and historical events, royal and papal commands, and occasional eulogies—is reflected to some extent in the syntactical categories of the subjunctives—in, for example, the high percentage of wishes (e.g., *ece him seo heofenlice iateward on heofenrice* [656]), in the frequent passages of indirect narrative (*bed him þet he scolde him giuen* . . . [963]), and in the numerous noun clauses following verbs expressing wish, command, desire, etc. (*ic wille . . . þet hit stande* [963]). The relatively small number of subjunctive modal structures in the *Chronicle,* compared to the number in *Melibee* (a difference, respectively, of 6.6 to 11.8 per cent per total finite verb structures), may be recognized more clearly as a stylistic influence if one takes into account the uneven distribution of subjunctive structures in the *Chronicle.* The subjunctives tend to appear in clusters, the entry for the year 675 alone showing thirty-four of the total of one hundred thirteen subjunctive modal forms. This entry, which gives a detailed account of the royal establishment of a monastery and the papal bull dealing with the monastic order and its duties, illustrates both the use of certain categories of subjunctives in such formal edicts and the high incidence of subjunctives in passages not restricted to the merely "factual" orientation of so much of the *Chronicle* (e.g., *Her forðferde Cnut cyng* . . . [1036]).

Whereas the *Chronicle* is, for the most part, a more-or-less factual statement of actual happenings, the two Chaucer tales are specifically "literary" in genre. As units in a dramatic presentation that ranges through the different social levels of the time, the individual tales reflect, to an extent, the speech of characters typical of the social levels they represent. *Melibee,* told by a learned narrator, has as its protagonists the "myghty and riche", Melibeus, and his obviously erudite wife, Prudence. Though voluble and argumentative, Prudence speaks ostensibly as the submissive wife and so is wont to preface her remarks with concessive statements (e.g., *But though attempree wepyng be ygraunted* [line 989]) , or to speak conditionally (. . . *if thou wene sikerly that the biwreiyng of thy conseil to a persone wol make thy condicion to stonden in the bettre plyt, thanne shaltou tellen hym thy conseil in this wise.* [line 1147])—not to mention her habit of quoting the ancient authorities. Interestingly, the two syntactic categories of concessive and conditional account for forty-six of the seventy-four subjunctive modal constructions found in the portion of the original texts included in this research.

The Parson's Tale, though a monologue on the nature of penitence rather than an argument, is purportedly narrated by a person of lower social standing, and one who is impassioned but unassuming in manner. The Parson's syntax, like Prudence's, is "deferential" (concessive and conditional subjunctives account for twenty-three of the total thirty-seven subjunctive modal structures in the portion of the original text subjected to analysis); but he also speaks in a rather less formal style, so that the total number of subjunctive modal forms found in his tale is only half the number found in *Melibee.*

A further stylistic—and linguistic—contrast is found in the number and type of non-distinctive subjunctive forms exhibited in the two tales, *Melibee* showing a total of fifteen, *The Parson's Tale* only two. The principal reason for the difference is the rather consistent use by Prudence of the polite plural form *ye,* which shows an ambiguous plural form of the subjunctive (e.g., . . . *if ye governe yow by sapience* . . . [*line* 993]), whereas the Parson, when proposing conditions, uses the familiar singular form *thou* (e.g., *If thou hast desdayn of thy servant* . . . [line 149]), or more frequently, the impersonal third person singular form (e.g., *"The firste is that if a man be baptized after that he hath sinned* . . ." [line 95]).

The translations of the three texts considered in this chapter are so faithful and so literal that their language often seems more typical of early Modern English than of present-day usage: e.g., . . . *be it never so often* (*The Parson's Tale* [line 90]); *And were it the lowest churl* . . . (*The Parson's Tale* [line 146]). The high totals of subjunctives and structures of modality that these translations show contrast with the much lower totals in the present-day English used in biblical translations (Chapter Two) or contemporary dramatic works (Chapter Five), and mark the translations as consciously "literary" works, written at a level of usage that still deliberately retains the subjunctive (as noted by Curme, Zandvoort, and others) .[3] Perhaps no feature indicates more clearly the conservatism of the translators than their occasional use of a subjunctive to translate constructions that do not use a subjunctive in the original text.

Though their literalness is probably the most obvious single feature of these translations, it is not the only or the most significant feature to be considered in tracing the pattern of subjunctive usage. The statistics shown in Table 6 and the examples given above illustrate the fact that the literal translations result in far fewer alternations of non-subjunctive–subjunctive constructions between texts than were found in the biblical translations. The textual evidence also shows fewer alternating constructions within the individual texts, with only the original *Chronicle* showing variation in identical structures.

However, close inspection of the textual evidence for the purpose of interpreting internal linguistic influences reveals numerous problems in modal designation, problems that arise largely because of the falling together of inflectional endings and because of the use of structures that are ambiguous as to modal type or syntactic category.

A list of indicative verb forms in the *Chronicle* that show non-distinctive *(–en)* endings is given in Appendix B, as are designations of subjunctive modal forms in *The Parson's Tale*. Further examples of alternating constructions within and between texts, and of structures ambiguous as to modality or to categorical classification follow below:

1. *Alternation in Structures within a Text.* Alternation

of subjunctive–indicative forms in expressing relative clauses is shown in the *Chronicle* in an entry for the year 675, which uses first the indicative verb structure *& hwa swa hit tobreceð . . .* , and later the subjunctive structures *& ic amansumie ealle þa þær aniþing ofbreke & ic bletsie ealle þa þe hit healden.*

2. *Alternation in Structures between Texts.* The most interesting type of alternation in structures between texts is that in which a subjunctive form in the translation contrasts with a non-subjunctive form in the original. Instances of such alternation appear in all three translations. The translation of the *Chronicle,* in contrast with the original, uses a subjunctive in the protasis of a conditional clause, the conditions of which seem quite possible; the original text and the translation are as follows:

> *Gif hwa hit doð (ðes papa curs of Rome & ealre biscope curs he habbe.)*
> *If anyone do so (may he have the curse of the pope . . .)*
> (675)

Again, in a relative clause, the translation shows a modal auxiliary construction contrasting with an indicative verb structure in the original:

> *Ic wille & tyde þæt whilc man swa haved behaten to faren to Rome . . .*
> *I desire and grant that whatever man may have made a vow to make a pilgrimage to Rome . . .* (675)

Even more unusual is the apparent reversal of the chronological pattern of modal development in the original and the translation of *Melibee,* when the translator uses a noun clause with a modal-auxiliary type subjunctive construction to translate an infinitive phrase:

*At alle tymes thou shalt blesse God, and praye hym to
dresse thy weyes . . .*

*Bless the Lord thy God always and desire of Him that
thy ways may be directed . . .* (line 1118)

Similar constructions are used in the translation of *The
Parson's Tale,* when the translator uses a noun clause with
a subjunctive verb form to translate an infinitive phrase,
and elsewhere, in contrast with the original, uses a subjunctive in a conditional protasis that states quite possible
conditions:

If thou hast desdayn of thy servant . . .
If thou have disdain for thy servant . . . (line 149)

*3. Use of Structures of Modality in Texts and Transla-
tions.* The use of modal auxiliary forms in all three texts
and translations is so frequent as to be unexceptional
save in the structures that are ambiguous. Modal auxiliary
constructions used in *The Parson's Tale* are listed and
discussed in Appendix B. More significant than the use
of modal auxiliary constructions in tracing the subjunctive pattern in the late Old and Middle English texts is
the early use of modal preterite constructions (as noted by
Blain in his monograph on the *Chronicle*).[4] Modal preterite forms in the *Chronicle* appear in both indirect narrative structures and conditional clauses:

. . . gerædde se cyng . . . þæt man gegaderode þa scipu . . .
. . . king . . . decided that all the ships should be collected.
(992)
*. . . þa wolden drohtien here lif on anker setle gif hi wisten
hwere . . .*
*. . . who would like to spend their lives in an anchorites
cell if they knew where . . .* (656)

In the late Middle English selections, the preterite forms

appear frequently in conditional clauses (e.g., "... *if I governed me by thy conseil, it sholde seme* ..." [*Melibee*, line 1057]), and appear also in concessive clauses in syntactic patterns that are markedly similar to present-day English usage:

> *Though I wiste that neither God ne man ne sholde never knowe it,* ...
> *Though I knew that neither God nor man should ever be cognizant of it,* ... (*The Parson's Tale,* line 143).

4. *Ambiguous Structures.* The sentence quoted above (*The Parson's Tale,* line 143) also illustrates a major problem encountered in classifying structures according to syntactic category. Though listed as concessive, the sentence could also be construed as conditional. Still more difficult to classify are the formulaic clauses that are used in the *Chronicle* to express royal or papal commands concerning the monasteries:

> & *swa ic hit freo þet nan biscop ne have þær nane hæse* ...
> *and in such wise I exempt it that no bishop shall have any authority there* ... (963)

In this book such clauses were classified in the result category, though the idea of purpose is also implicit in the expression. In contrast, the following construction in *Melibee* was classed as a purpose clause, though it may be argued that the clause also implies result:

> *we conseille that* ... *thou sette sufficeant garnisoun so that they may* ... *defende* ...
> *we counsel that* ... *you establish a sufficient garrison, so that the house may be as well defended as you yourself* ... (line 1027)

Also ambiguous as to syntactic category was the following subjunctive structure in *Melibee:*

> *for the whiche resouns it were a ful greet peril to erren in this matiere;*
>
> *For all these reasons it were dangerous indeed to err in this matter;* (line 1024) .

This structure was classified as "conjectural" under an *ad hoc* category (numbered 14) that was used in classifying certain subjunctive forms found in the texts considered in this chapter and in Chapters IV and V.

For the most part, ambiguous modal structures were found in passages in which a modal auxiliary construction was used, as in the following noun clause from the *Chronicle:*

> *(wile þes geornen) þæt we moten þær wircen an mynstre . . .*
>
> *(I desire) that we may build there a monastery . . .* (656).

Since the substitute frame "That we [he] build there a monastery" is ambiguous in meaning, the structure was classed as a non-distinctive subjunctive.

In *Melibee,* the periphrastic constructions in the conditional sentence,

> *. . . if ye wol triste to my conseil, I shal restoore you your doghter hool . . .*
>
> *. . . If you will trust to my advice, I will restore to you . . .* (line 1109),

were classified as modal auxiliary constructions, since the substitute frame is not ambiguous, even though the temporal connotations of the auxiliary forms are obvious. However, the periphrastic construction in the conditional clause,

> *. . . and if ye wole werken wikkednesse . . .*
> *. . . And if your will is to work wickedness . . .* (line
> 1091),

was designated as non-subjunctive, since a different meaning (of actuality rather than intention) is conveyed by the substitute frame "If ye werken . . ."

In summary, a comparative analysis of the originals and translations of certain late Old English and late Middle English secular writings reveals the following patterns of subjunctive usage:

1. Total subjunctive modal structures show a decline in frequency in present-day English translations, but the decline is far less marked than that shown in the present-day biblical translation. However, in contrast to original texts, the translations exhibit a radical decline—upwards of 200 per cent—in the use of inflected subjunctives.

2. The present-day translations show a pattern of almost exact inversion with original texts in relative percentages of subjunctives and of modal auxiliary constructions per total modal structures. This pattern of inversion indicates (a) a marked increase in the use of modal auxiliary forms and (b) the fact that, even in deliberately conservative, "literary" writings, the inflected subjunctive tends to give way to the periphrastic structure. Modal preterite inflections show a marked increase in usage in both Middle and present-day English, both original texts and translations showing almost equal percentages of usage per total modal structures.

3. Statistically, the incidence of non-distinctive subjunctive structures reached a peak in both numerical frequency and percentage of usage in a Middle English text, and a sub-peak in the late Old English text. The high percentage of non-distinctive forms in both texts is attrib-

utable in large part to the falling together of inflectional endings. In the Middle English text *Melibee,* the stylistic use of the polite second person plural form *(ye),* rather than the familiar singular form *(thou),* accounts for the higher percentage of non-distinctive forms in this text as compared with the less formal writing in the Middle English text *The Parson's Tale.*

4. Among the non-subjunctive forms used in either an original text or its translation in contrast with a subjunctive form in the compared text, the constructions most frequently found are indicative mood forms and infinitive phrases. Significant patterns of alternation according to syntactic category of the subjunctive structure are as follows: (a) frequent alternation of indicative mood forms with subjunctives used in indirect narrative and in noun clauses, and (b) in the translation of the *Chronicle,* frequent use of infinitives in translating indirect narration.

5. Apart from the influence of the conservative, literal nature of the translations on the subjunctive patterns exhibited in them, certain external linguistic influences (such as literary genre, style, and subject matter) seem to have had pronounced effects. That is, the more formal, literary texts show a higher percentage of subjunctive forms than do the non-literary or less literary, less formal texts.

Chapter Four

Middle English Dialects

Tᴇɴ ᴛᴇxᴛs,* ɪɴᴄʟᴜᴅɪɴɢ ᴇxᴀᴍ-
ples of prose and poetry from each of the five Middle English dialects, were compared in an effort to discover
whether dialectal variations in subjunctive usage patterns
existed, and if so, what they were. However, the statistical
evidence (displayed in Tables 7 and 8) reveals no clear-
cut or particularly significant patterns. Quite to the con-

*The texts considered in this chapter, grouped according to
dialectal division, are the following:
   Northern
   1. *Cursor Mundi* (MS Cotton Vespasian A 3) *ca.* 1340 [*ca.*
1325].
   2. *The Form of Living* (MS Cambridge Dd V 64) *ca.* 1400
[*ca.* 1343–*ca.* 1349].

trary, both the statistics and, even more clearly, the textual evidence reveal a marked inconsistency in usage within as well as between dialects, and even within individual texts. In sum, the evidence tends to confirm the results of a study of the subjunctive in conditional clauses, made by Asta Kihlboom in 1939, and Kihlboom's conclusion to the effect that there was indeed a tendency in Middle English to level modal usage under either indicative or subjunctive, but that the levelings did not seem to follow any demonstrable dialectal lines (insofar as could be ascertained from syntactical evidence available to Kihlboom).[1]

East Midland

3. *Peterborough Chronicle* (MS Bodley Laud 636, last hand) *ca.* 1160 [*ca.* 1160].

4. *Havelok the Dane* (MS Bodley Laud Misc. 108) *ca.* 1325 [*ca.* 1300].

West Midland

5. *Hali Meidenhad* (MS Bodley 34) *ca.* 1225 [*ca.* 1200?].

6. *Sir Gawain and the Green Knight* (MS Cotton Nero A 10) *ca.* 1400 [1390–1400?].

Southeastern

7. *Poema Morale* (MS Bodley Digby A 4) *ca.* 1250? [*ca.* 1175].

8. *Ayenbit of Inwyt* (MS Arundel 57) *ca.* 1350 [1340].

Southwestern

9. *Poema Morale* (MS Egerton 613, fol. 7) *ca.* 1250? [*ca.* 1175?].

10. *John of Trevisa's Trans. of Ralph Higden's Polychronicon* (MS St. John's College Cambridge H 1) *ca.* 1400 [*ca.* 1387].

Textual sampling was restricted to the first 500–plus finite verbs in the texts, with the following exceptions in which 500–plus verbs were selected: *Cursor Mundi*, lines 4955–5470; *Peterborough Chronicle*, entries 1123–1135, line 9; *Ayenbit of Inwyt*, p. 11, line 24, p. 19, line 32 ("The Tenth Commandment"); p. 57, line 13, p. 60, line 20 ("The Sins of the Tongue"); *John of Trevisa's Trans.*, Vol. I, Chapter XI: p. 79, line 4, p. 125, line 3. The variation in sampling technique in the final text was made to determine whether the unusually limited use of subjunctives was representative of the entire text. The totals of subjunctive structures found in the portion of each text required to furnish 500 non-subjunctive finite verbs are listed in the statistics given in Table 7.

However, in certain specific details the dialectal analysis does tend to substantiate certain patterns that were noted in the diachronic comparisons reported in earlier chapters, i.e., patterns relative particularly to types of modal constructions and to variations in usage influenced by literary style and subject matter.

The most important of these patterns, and the one best substantiated by the statistics, is the frequency of both modal auxiliary constructions and modal preterite inflections. With only two exceptions—both of them in relatively early texts, *Hali Meidenhad* and *Ayenbit of Inwyt*—structures of modality account for at least 40 per cent of all subjunctive modal structures found in the texts. Higher percentages of modal preterite inflections are shown in the Southern texts.

A second significant pattern is shown in the high percentage of non-distinctive subjunctive structures in each translation, with an average percentage of 24.5 per total subjunctive structures and extremes of 9.5 per cent and 57.8 per cent. This high frequency of non-distinctive forms, comparable to that revealed in the diachronic analyses of Middle English texts, is directly attributable to the falling together of inflectional endings in the Central dialects and the partial loss of final *n* in both subjunctive and indicative forms in all dialects, as detailed in David Reed's study[2] (see Appendix A). The two texts in the Northern dialect show the highest percentages of non-distinctive subjunctive forms: *Cursor Mundi*, 57.8 per cent, *The Form of Living*, 34.6 per cent. By 1340, as Reed has observed, the Northern dialect had lost—or was in the process of losing—the *n* in preterite forms, in present subjunctive forms, and in present indicative forms immediately before or after personal pronoun subject forms.

While it is impossible on the basis of evidence furnished by such a restricted synchronic study to establish any definite patterns of subjunctive usage according to literary genre, it is possible to chart certain general features affected by genre, style, and subject matter. For example, of the five poetic texts analyzed, three of them—*Havelok the Dane, Poema Morale* (Digby), *Poema Morale* (Egerton) — show higher percentages of both inflected subjunctives and total subjunctive modal structures than are found in any of the prose texts. This fact would seem to support the notion, stated in an earlier chapter, that formal literary writing uses more subjunctives than less formal writing. However, the other poetic texts—*Gawain* and *Cursor Mundi*—show surprisingly low totals, ranking respectively eighth and tenth in percentage of inflected subjunctives and in percentage of total modal structures used.

If one considers style and subject matter as well as genre, it is easy to discover a plausible explanation for the relatively higher percentages of subjunctive usage in certain prose texts. Both of the two highest ranking ones— *Hali Meidenhad* and *The Form of Living*—are didactic in nature and include numerous conditional statements (e.g., *If þai saw þat, many of þam wold forsake all þat þai have . . . [The Form of Living*, p. 11]). Of the fifty-one subjunctive modal structures in *The Form of Living*, forty-five are in the conditional syntactic category; of the forty-nine subjunctive modal structures in *Hali Meidenhad*, twenty-two are in the conditional category.

Even superficial examination of the remaining texts illustrates the effects of subject matter on subjunctive usage. Among the four texts showing the highest percentage of subjunctive usage—*Havelok the Dane, Hali Meidenhad, Poema Morale* (Digby), and *Poema Morale* (Egerton)—the latter two are manuscripts of a didactic religious poem and show high totals of subjunctive constructions in the syntactic category of conditional clauses. They also show, in common with *Havelok the Dane,* high total of command category subjunctives. The texts showing the lowest percentages of subjunctive usage—*Cursor Mundi, Gawain, John of Trevisa's Trans.,* and *Ayenbit of Inwyt*—are, in the portions of the text analyzed, largely narrative or descriptive in subject and style, rather than didactic or argumentative.

While these hypotheses concerning the possible influence of style and of subject matter on subjunctive patterns are admittedly not based on strictly linguistic evidence, and are at least partially founded on subjective judgments, they do serve to support the contentions in an earlier chapter concerning the use of the subjunctive as a stylistic device (Chapter I, page 18). The existence of evidence of such influences and such usage patterns as early as the Middle English period helps to substantiate the chronological pattern of subjunctive decline, both generally and within specific syntactic categories. For example, the *Peterborough Chronicle,* which is in a style much less formal than *Havelok the Dane,* shows significant differences in both total subjunctive usage and usage by syntactic category (see Table 8, columns 3 and 4). A detailed study of each text would be necessary to trace individual patterns, but cursory examination indicates a more frequent use of subjunctive constructions in *Havelok* to express curses and wishes, to make comparative, concessive, and conditional statements, and to conjecture about temporal events.

On the basis of the purely linguistic evidence, however, the most prominent finding of the dialectal analysis is the frequent inconsistency in modality mentioned earlier in this chapter. Even manuscripts of the same poem (e.g., *Poema Morale* [Digby] and *Poema Morale* [Egerton]) show variation in the types of modal structures employed. Still more indicative of a general inconsistency in the linguistic means used to express modality are the variations in identical structures within a text and the high percentages of atypical and ambiguous structures. Some of the internal linguistic influences that affected the developmental pattern of the subjunctive in the Middle English period are illustrated by the following examples:

1. *Alternation in Structures between Texts.* Typical of the variations between the two manuscripts of the *Poema Morale* texts is this temporal construction in which the Digby MS uses an indicative form in contrast with a subjunctive form in the Egerton MS:

> . . . *þer wile hi bieð a live.* (Digby, 1. 62)
> . . . *þe wyle he bo alife.* (Egerton, 1. 30)

The manuscripts also show variation in type of modal structure as in the following comparative clause in which the Digby MS uses the past tense subjunctive form and the Egerton MS uses the present tense subjunctive:

> . . . *swich hit were on boc iwrite* (Digby, 1. 222)
> . . . *swilc it seie on boc i-writen* (Egerton, 1. 117)

In the following conditional clauses, the Digby MS has periphrastic preterite forms and the Egerton MS has modal preterite inflections. (However, both constructions were designated as modal preterite inflections for purposes of statistical analysis. See Appendix A.)

> *Ef we wolden herie gode swo we doð arminges*
> *We mihten richu be . . .* (Digby, line 618)
> *ȝif we serveden god so we doð erninges*
> *More we haveden of hevene . . .* (Egerton, line 319)

2. *Alternations in Structures within a Text.* Examples are to be found in almost every text but are especially numerous in the Northern and Midland selections. In the *Cursor Mundi,* the frequent omission of *–e* in subjunctives of the wish–curse category makes it necessary to classify most such structures as non-distinctive, as in the following three examples (of which only the first was classified as subjunctive) :

> *Godd give him his brad blissing!* (line 5334)
> *He sceild him fra his wither-win!* (line 5366)
> *Ur laverd us grant to end him with.* (line 5466)

In the same work, two verbs used in a syntactic structure after a verb *(prai)* expressing wish, command, desire, and so forth, show variation:

> *And mine i þrai for-give yee now;*
> *For-gives me þat i did you tak . . .* (line 5078)

The first verb *(for-give)* was classed as non-distinctive: preceding (as it does) a personal subject pronoun, it lacks the normal ending and could be indicative, imperative, or subjunctive. The second verb *(for-gives),* since it shows the imperative plural ending *–es,* was classed as a non-subjunctive.

A similar variation may be seen in the Northern text *The Form of Living,* which has one non-distinctive sub-

junctive form and one inflected subjunctive in a parallel
structure expressing purpose:

> (. . . *þat aght to be our desyre, our prayer and our en-*
> *tent*) . . .
> *þat þe fyre of hys lufe kyndell our heart and þe swetnes*
> *of hys grace be our comforth* . . . (p. 9)

In the East Midland text *Havelok,* a similar omitting
of *–e* is shown in a clause of result in which the two verbs
in a compound structure vary:

> *(Of kniht ne hauede he neuere drede)*
> *þat he ne sprong forth* . . .
> *And lete him* ['*knawe*'] *of hise hand-dede.* (line 92)

The West Midland text *Hali Meidenhad* shows the
variation of indicative and subjunctive forms in a compound structure expressing result (e. g., . . . *swa þat ha
naveð nawt freo of hire selven ł trukie for a man of
lom þe hevenliche laverd* [p. 5, 36]) ; and the West Midland text *Gawain* shows the indicative–subjunctive alternation in the conditional clause:

> *If any so hardy in þis hous holdeȝ hymseluen,*
> *Be so bolde in his blod* . . . (line 285)

Even in the more frequently uniform Southeastern text
Ayenbit of Inwyt, variations appear in subjunctive structures used after impersonal constructions:

> *Hit behovede þet alle wenten into helle and þere*
> *abyde* . . . *ine zikere hope þet iesu crist godes zone ssolde*
> *come* . . . (pp. 12–13)

The forms *wenten* and *abyde* are non-distinctive; the
modal auxiliary construction *ssolde come* fits a pattern of
substitution ("in the hope that Christ *come*") and was

classified accordingly as a modal auxiliary type subjunctive.

3. *Use of Structures of Modality.* Most of the Middle English texts analyzed—the one exception is the West Midland text *Hali Meidenhad*—show a high percentage of modal auxiliary constructions, and also show (in Southern texts) a remarkably high percentage of modal preterite constructions. Typical of the latter, labeled according to textual source and syntactic category, are the following:

> *But als þai war knigthes rik; (Cursor Mundi,* line 5134)
> [comparison]

> *Yif scho coupe on horse ride, . . .*
> *And sho were comen in-til elde . . . (Havelock,* line 126)
> [conditional]

> *And as sadly þe segge hym in his sadel sette*
> *As non unhap had hym ayled, (þaʒ hedleʒ he were in*
>   *stedde.) (Gawain,* line 438)   [comparison]

> *. . . se devel self mihte habbe milce ef he hit bigunne.*
>   *(Poema Morale,* Digby MS. line 418)   [conditional]

4. *Atypical Subjunctive Structures.* Atypical subjunctive constructions sometimes show preservation of the older subjunctive endings and sometimes show interesting innovations or orthographical variations.

Among the most interesting orthographical variations are the contrasted spellings of the singular subjunctive form of the verb *be* in the *Poema Morale* (Egerton). Normally spelled *be,* the form appears as follows in the juxtaposed subjunctives that are of the command and the temporal categories, respectively:

> *. . . bue for him selve æfrech man þe wyle he bo alife.* (line
>   30)

Among the atypical structures not designated as sub-junctives are verbs identical to subjunctive forms but used in syntactical structures that normally show indica-tive forms. Such structures are illustrated in these excerpts from *Gawain* and *John of Trevisa's Trans.*:

þis watʒ kynges countenance where he in court were, ...
                                        (*Gawain*, line 100)

... þaʒ hedleʒ he were in stedde   (*Gawain*, line 438)

For uch wyʒe may wel wit no wont þat þer were.
                                        (*Gawain*, line 131)

And so it moot be, þat þere by tweye londes of byheste ...
    (translating: *ex quibus liquet aliam esse*)
                    (*John of Trevisa's Trans.*, p. 107, line 2)

5. *Ambiguous Structures.* In addition to the large num-ber of non-distinctive subjunctive forms in the Middle English texts (see sub-totals, Table 7), textual analysis reveals higher percentages of ambiguous structures than are to be found in either the biblical or the secular writ-ings discussed in the preceding chapters. Reasons for con-sidering a structure ambiguous range from problems of syntactical classification to uncertainty about the likeli-hood of a patriarch addressing God in the imperative. Examples of structures difficult to classify as to syntactic category are shown in the following from the *Peter-borough Chronicle:*

(... behet him ... þæt gif he moste Engle lond secen
    þet he scolde begeton hem þone mynstre of Burch.)
    swa þæt he scolde setten þær prior of Clunni ... &
    ealle þa þing ... he scolde him betæcen.   (1131)

The last two subjunctive constructions *(scolde setten* and *scolde betæcen)* were classified in the purpose category though it may well be argued that they also denote result. This structure from *Hali Meidenhad*, classified as conditional, might equally well be classified as a concessive type subjunctive:

> *Meidenhad is tresor þat beo hit eanes forloren (ne beð hit neaver ifunden . . .)* (p. 11, line 18).

Among the constructions listed in the *ad hoc* category was the following one from *Gawain;* conjectural in nature, it is similar to the conditional category subjunctive in proposing a hypothetical condition or supposition:

> *þat were to tor for to telle of tryfles þe halve . . .* (line 165).

Similar to this structure in expressing a supposition is the following construction from *Hali Meidenhad*, also placed in the *ad hoc* category:

> *. . . wel were ham weren ha on hare brudlakes dei iboren to biburien . . .* (p. 9, line 22)

Finally, the problem of classifying verbs in the patriarch Jacob's appeals to God *(Cursor Mundi)* is at least a subjective one if not a theological one. In the speech

> *"Laverd . . . Savve mi childir hole to me*
> *And have a ioseph saule pite!"* (line 5034)

the verbs in form may be either subjunctive, normal in invoking the Deity, or imperative. Since in tone, at any rate, the address seems imperative, the verbs were classified as non-distinctive subjunctive forms under the category of wish–curse.

In summary, a comparison of the Middle English dialects reveals the following patterns of subjunctive usage:

1. No significant patterns of variation in usage of the subjunctive according to dialectal division are apparent.

There is, instead, a general inconsistency in expressing modality both between texts and within particular texts.

2. In specific details, the dialect study does substantiate certain facts noted earlier in diachronic investigations of the English subjunctive. A consistent and marked increase in use of structures of modality is evident, since in nine of ten texts investigated, modal auxiliary constructions or modal preterite inflections account for 30 per cent or more of the total subjunctive structures. Modal preterite inflections are much more numerous in texts of the Southeastern and Southwestern dialects. The uniformly high percentages of non-distinctive subjunctive constructions (with an average percentage of 24.5 for the ten texts) indicate the direct effect on modal distinction of the leveled inflections of the Middle English period.

3. Statistics of the dialect study substantiate the hypothesis that subjunctive usage is directly related to literary genre, since the more "literary" texts consistently show significantly higher percentages of subjunctive usage than non-belletristic works. The influence of subject matter seems also to be directly reflected in subjunctive usage, since didactic or argumentative literature shows a greater percentage of subjunctive usage than narrative or descriptive literature.

4. Internal linguistic influences, as shown in textual evidence, reveal both the numerous changes and the frequent inconsistencies in the forms used to indicate modality during the Middle English period. Changes are illustrated by the increasing use of structures of modality, particularly the modal preterite inflections; inconsistencies are illustrated by variations in the means used to indicate modality both between and within texts, and by ambiguous and atypical modal forms.

Chapter Five

Dramatic Texts

$\mathbf{D}$ESCRIPTIVE ANALYSIS OF THE
subjunctive patterns and other grammatical characteristics
found in twenty-four British and American dramatic
works, spanning a period of more than five centuries, provides further evidence of a radical decline in subjunctive
usage.*

*The twenty-four texts, ranging in date from 1430–40 to 1961,
are listed below, grouped chronologically in pairs (e.g., one and
two, three and four, five and six, etc.). Four texts, numbered 15a,
16a, 19a, and 20a, and enclosed in brackets, are *not* included in
the statistical analysis reported in Tables 9 and 10 and Figure 5, but
they are treated in Table 11. These supplemental texts were compared with the ones immediately preceding (e.g., 15a with 15, 16a
with 16, etc.). Dates in brackets are those of composition or first
performance (when different from MS or publication date).

Perhaps the most striking feature of the statistics displayed here (see Tables 9, 10, and 11, and Figure 5) is the marked similarity of the subjunctive patterns found in the dramatic texts to the patterns found in the biblical translations discussed in Chapter Two. The texts in both groups show an almost uninterrupted decline in the use of

---

1. 1430–40 *Harrowing of Hell* [1340–50] (York Cycle)
2. 1475 *Noah* [1400] (Towneley Cycle)
3. 1566 *Ralph Roister Doister* [1553–54] (Nicholas Udall)
4. 1562 Gorboduc [1560] (Thomas Norton and Thomas Sackville)
5. 1604 *Doctor Faustus* [1589] (Christopher Marlowe)
6. 1623 *Two Gentlemen of Verona* [1591] (William Shakespeare)
7. 1676 *The Man of Mode* (Sir George Etherege)
8. 1678 *All For Love* (John Dryden)
9. 1723 *The Conscious Lovers* [1722] (Sir Richard Steele)
10. 1731 *The London Merchant* (George Lillo)
11. 1773 *She Stoops to Conquer* (Oliver Goldsmith)
12. 1777 *The School for Scandal* (Richard Sheridan)
13. 1815 *The Three Doctors* (Thomas Peacock)
14. 1824 *Charles the Second* (J. H. Payne and W. Irving)
15. 1877 *Harold* (Alfred Lord Tennyson)
[15a. 1893 *The Second Mrs. Tanqueray* (Sir Arthur Pinero)]
16. 1880 *Hazel Kirke* (J. S. MacKaye)
[16a. 1897 *Shenandoah* [1888] (Bronson Howard)]
17. 1929 *The Sacred Flame* (W. Somerset Maugham)
18. 1922 *The Hairy Ape* (Eugene O'Neill)
19. 1959 *A Taste of Honey* (Shelagh Delaney)
[19a. 1961 *A Subject of Scandal and Concern* (John Osborne)]
20. 1949 *Death of a Salesman* (Arthur Miller)
[20a. 1947 *Command Decision* [1946] (W. W. Haines)]

Textual sampling of all but one of the works was restricted to the first 500–plus verbs required to furnish five hundred non-subjunctive verb structures. The exception was made in the case of the earliest play, *Harrowing of Hell,* for which the entire text was used and only three hundred and sixty non-subjunctive verb forms plus forty-one subjunctive modal structures were analyzed. In all cases the sampling was restricted to dialogue only.

inflected subjunctive forms, almost to the vanishing point in present-day usage.

Secondly, a similar decline in the use of all types of subjunctive modal structures is also indicated. In the first four texts (fifteenth and sixteenth centuries) the average usage of subjunctive modal structures per total finite verb forms is 7.4 per cent; in the last four (twentieth century) the comparable percentage is only 2.4.

A third pattern (not revealed so clearly in the biblical investigation, partly for reasons of content) is the amazingly high incidence of preterite modal inflections as indicators of subjunctive mood. This usage is particularly evident in British (as contrasted with American) English, the modal preterite inflections accounting for 81.2 per cent of all subjunctive structures in one of the two twentieth-century British plays analyzed, and 100 per cent of such structures in the other.

In addition to these three general patterns, a number of secondary but nonetheless significant patterns were encountered. They involve variation in usage according to chronological period, dialect, genre of textual material, and syntactic category of the subjunctive structures. Statistics for the two late nineteenth-century texts (Table 9, columns 15 and 16) indicate a slight upswing in frequency of subjunctive structures and a more pronounced increase in the percentage of inflected subjunctives. Statistics for American dramatic texts (columns 14, 16, 18, and 20) reveal, with one exception, a higher incidence of inflected subjunctive forms than the corresponding British texts (columns 13, 15, 17, and 19), and a markedly smaller proportion of modal preterite inflections. Patterns of usage according to syntactic category of the subjunctive (see Table 9) show a surprising consistency among all of the texts in the use of subjunctives in the following categories: (a) wish–curse, (b) noun clauses after verbs of saying, thinking, wishing, commanding, etc., and (c) conditional statements. Through the mid-eighteenth century, consistent usage is shown also in the categories of comparison, concession, time, and purpose. Finally, when comparison of literary genre or style was possible—i.e., comparison of the "formal" language of tragedies and the relatively "informal" language of comedies—higher percentages of subjunctive usage were found in the tragedies.

The incidence of non-distinctive subjunctives, though uniformly high in the two late Middle English texts, follows no significant or consistent pattern in the Modern English texts. The two most significant general patterns indicated by these statistics (i.e., the decline in usage of both the inflected subjunctive and of all types of subjunctive modal structures) follow and confirm the description of the subjunctive given in historical studies, already discussed at some length in Chapter One. However, when interpreting the more specific patterns (i.e., variation according to chronological period, dialect, and style, and consistency in usage according to syntactic category) it is necessary to take note of a number of external and internal influences, linguistic and otherwise. Detailed examination of statistics and of textual evidence also helps illustrate a pattern that is uniquely evident in the dramatic texts: the surprisingly high frequency of modal preterite inflections in present-day English.

Variation in subjunctive usage over time, and specifically the increase in usage late in the nineteenth century, confirms in some measure a statement by Jespersen, quoted earlier in this study, to the effect that beginning in mid-nineteenth century there was a literary revival of some of the subjunctive uses.[1] Statistics for the two plays of this period (columns 15 and 16), in addition to showing an increase in both total subjunctive structures and inflected subjunctives, reveal the use of subjunctive structures in the syntactic categories of purpose and result clauses—a pattern that is exceptional in post-seventeenth century dramatic texts in result clauses, and exceptional in purpose clauses after mid-eighteenth century. Both plays show a uniformly high frequency in the syntactic categories that were most frequently found in all dramatic texts examined, namely (a) wish–curse, (b) noun clauses after verbs of saying, thinking, wishing, commanding, etc., and (c) conditional statements.

Particularly germane to Jespersen's observation is Tennyson's play *Harold* (column 15). Classified as a tragedy, this work also provides evidence for the notion that literary genre influences—or is at least related to—variation in modal structures. The factor of style, far from preventing the play from fitting Jespersen's thesis as being atypical, instead qualifies it, since its formal style meets more nearly Jespersen's restriction to "literary" writing than does the more conversational style of the second play of this period, the American romantic comedy *Hazel Kirke*. Textual analysis of Tennyson's tragedy reveals more fully the formal, almost archaic nature of the dialogue used. Not only does Tennyson use such subjunctive structures as ". . . and be the king so wise,—Then Tostig too were wiser than he seems" (20),[2] and ". . . Side not with Tostig in any violence/Lest thou be sideways guilty of the violence" (28), but also he uses what Jespersen has termed the archaic indicative *be*,[3] as in the interrogative clause, "Be there not fair woods and fields in England . . ." (20).

At this point it is necessary to mention certain facts (in

addition to the obvious limitations of the statistics) that prevent any unqualified statement as to a definite increase in subjunctive usage late in the nineteenth century. The second late nineteenth-century play analyzed is an American text and, frequently, the American texts show slightly higher percentages of subjunctives. Further, the twentieth-century plays (columns 17, 18, 19, and 20), far from indicating a continuation of subjunctive revival, indicate an increasingly sharp decline. Finally, there is the possibility, indeed the probability, that Tennyson used subjunctive (and other archaic) structures to suggest the linguistic patterns of the historical period (the eleventh century) in which his tragedy is set.

However, the statistics of the supplementary texts investigated in order to ascertain whether or not Tennyson's drama was unique in its linguistic patterns offer further support for Jespersen's belief that there was a revival in subjunctive usage late in the nineteenth century. (The texts are numbered 15a and 16a, Table 11.) The English play, a drama of social criticism entitled *The Second Mrs. Tanqueray,* while showing fewer inflected subjunctives than Tennyson's *Harold,* does show a high percentage of total subjunctive modal structures per total finite verbs. Similarly, the American text of this period, a Civil War drama entitled *Shenandoah,* while having very few inflected subjunctives, shows a rather high proportion of subjunctive modal structures.

Variation in subjunctive usage according to dialect is confirmed by statistics from a greater number of texts than is variation by chronological period. Of the four American texts analyzed, three show a higher percentage of inflected subjunctive usage than the corresponding British texts, and two show a higher percentage of total subjunctive structures. (See Table 11, columns 14, 16, 18, 20 [American], and columns 13, 15, 17, 19 [British].) Beyond the relatively limited statistics, the texts involved in the comparison lend considerable support to the hypothesis of dialectal variation. One of the English texts ranking higher in both percentage of inflected subjunctives and total subjunctive structures is *Harold*, discussed above as atypical in subjunctive usage; this tragedy shows, in fact, subjunctive usage percentages considerably higher than any other British text after 1731.

A second influence, operative in the other contrasted pair of texts in which the British play shows higher subjunctive usage, concerns the subject matter and literary style of the two texts. Most of the characters in O'Neill's *The Hairy Ape* are relatively uneducated ship workers, and the dialogue reflects their conversation. In contrast, the characters in the British text, Maugham's *The Sacred Flame*, are wealthy and highly educated Britishers. The conversation in the O'Neill play, limited almost entirely in the section analyzed to the workers' arguments and discussions, consists of rhapsodic eulogies and blasphemous indictments of the seaman's plight. In a total of eleven subjunctive structures found in the O'Neill play, not one conditional subjunctive is listed (although seven curses are), as contrasted with the Maugham play in which five of a total of seventeen subjunctive structures occur in conditional statements made by two of the protagonists while playing chess. In addition, two structures in the American play were designated as non-distinctive subjunctive forms, since they occur in the speech of non-native speakers of English and are, therefore, ambiguous.

Variation of subjunctive usage according to dialect is particularly evident in the numbers and percentages rela-

tive to modal type of the subjunctive structures (see sub-
totals in Table 9 and percentages according to modal type,
Table 10). Uniformly, the American texts among the first
twenty that were analyzed show higher percentages of
inflected subjunctives—significantly higher in all contrasting pairs except the one in which the British text is
Harold (column 15). Twentieth-century American texts
also show a significantly lower percentage of modal preterite inflections than do British texts of the same decade
(11.1 per cent to 81.2 per cent, 53.8 per cent to 100 per
cent, respectively). In usage according to the syntactic
categories of the subjunctives, no significant difference between British and American texts is discernible, other
than the one already mentioned (i.e., the absence of conditional structures in *The Hairy Ape*) and a consistently
higher usage of wish–curse subjunctives in the American
texts.

The two supplementary twentieth-century texts (i.e.,
19a and 20a) do not indicate the dialectal variation quite
so clearly. This may be explained in part by differences in
style and subject matter that can be seen by comparing
these two with earlier plays. The texts show similar percentages of subjunctive modal structures per total finite
verbs (see Table 11). The only inflected subjunctive in
either text is in the British work; textual investigation
shows that it is a formulaic structure used in an editorializ-
ing newspaper story: "To their lasting shame, *be it spoken,*
a considerable portion of the company applauded these
profane opinions" (*A Subject of Scandal and Concern*,
17). Textual investigation also reveals that eight of the
eighteen subjunctives appearing in the British text are of
the polite usage category and that all are part of the
legal language used in the pre-trial and trial scenes of the

drama (e.g., *"Would you mind* one more question, Mr. Holyoake?" [*A Subject of Scandal and Concern,* 16]).

Unique in the statistics of the American text is the high (94.1 per cent) frequency of modal preterite inflections, an incidence that compares more nearly with British English texts than with other American texts (with the single exception of *Shenandoah,* the other supplementary text analyzed, which shows a rate of 95.3 per cent modal preterite inflections). These percentages, along with 53.2 per cent usage of modal preterite inflections in the post-World War II drama *Death of a Salesman* (column 20, Table 10), support the hypothesis that dramatic textual material shows a preference for the modal preterite construction in both British and American usage. However, the higher percentage of modal preterite inflections in four of the six British texts—higher compared to the American plays—supports the assumption that British English shows an even higher usage of the construction.

Variation in subjunctive usage according to genre or literary style is confirmed by the statistics of the four sets of plays that afford contrast between tragedy and comedy. (The contrasted texts are numbered as follows in the Tables, with the comedy listed first in each pair: columns 3 and 4, 7 and 8, 9 and 10, 16 and 15.) Three of the tragedies (a) show a significantly higher percentage of subjunctive structures per total finite verbs, and (b) show slightly higher percentages of inflected subjunctives. With one exception, the tragedies show no marked contrast with comedies in usage by syntactic category. The exception is *Harold,* which shows certain exceptional usages in the categories of time and result.

The increased frequency of subjunctive structures in the dramatic texts classed as tragedies follows and reconfirms the pattern of increased usage in formal literary writing discussed in Chapters 3 and 4. The language in dramatic texts from the fifteenth through the nineteenth centuries reflects the extremely formal style considered appropriate to tragedy. However, it is interesting to observe that the last four dramatic texts analyzed, all of which might be called "modern tragedies" (except, perhaps, Maugham's *The Sacred Flame*), differ from earlier tragedies as much linguistically as they do in style and subject matter. The dialogue in all four plays—but particularly in *The Hairy Ape, Death of a Salesman*, and *A Taste of Honey*—purports to be colloquial and idiomatic, quite different in style from the formal, "elevated" speech of such texts as *Gorboduc* and *Harold*. Obviously, such a stylistic difference is not central to the present study, but it must be noted, at least, in order to explain the sharp contrast in linguistic patterns. The stylistic change further supports the thesis advanced earlier that the subjunctive, even in its modern guise of structures of modality, is used much more frequently in formal literature, such as the translations of Chaucer discussed in Chapter Three, than it is in the deliberately non-literary language of most contemporary drama.

Like certain usage patterns in the Chaucer tales, the pattern of consistency of subjunctive usage in certain syntactic categories—namely (1) wish–curse, (2) noun clauses after verbs of saying, thinking, wishing, commanding, etc., and (3) conditional statements—can be partly explained in terms of the nature of the subject matter, both generally and in specific texts. The category that always shows the highest percentage of usage—the conditional statement—is used frequently and of necessity by protagonists in plays as they argue, prophesy, and review the involvements and action of the drama. The structure is as necessary to the twentieth-century Willy Loman of *Death of a Salesman* ("If old man Wagner was alive . . . I'd a been in charge of New York now. . . ." [1064]) as it was to George Barnwell, protagonist of the eighteenth-century play *The London Merchant* ("Yet had you been less indulgent, I had been most wretched . . ." [line 150, 644]). In the latter play, twenty-six of the thirty-eight subjunctive structures found were of the conditional variety.

The other syntactic category that shows a high incidence and a consistent pattern of usage is that of wish—curse. Interestingly, the textual evidence reveals a developing preference for curses over wishes. In the early plays expressions of wish are quite frequent: "Now blissid be He . . ." (*Noah,* line 467), and curses are expressed rather formally: ". . . *all ill mot þou spede!" (Harrowing of Hell,* line 139). Progressively in later dramatic works, curses seem to become more popular, e.g., in *Faustus,* "Aye, take it, and the devil give thee good on it, . . ."; and also shorter, as in *The Man of Mode:* "Damn her, dunghill", until in modern drama they develop into structures that (as Jespersen points out[4]) almost fit the pattern of a noun, e.g., Willy Loman's frequent *goddammit's.*

More than subjunctive structures in any other syntactic category, those of the wish—curse type tend to distort the pattern of modal usage in several of the dramatic texts investigated. Even a cursory examination of the sub-totals for Category 1 in Table 9 reveals surprising variations of forms in this classification. Only two texts, *The School for Scandal* and *A Taste of Honey,* reveal no wish—curse structures in the evidence considered. Other texts reveal such high percentages as *Noah,* in which nineteen of the fifty-three structures listed are of the wish—curse type, and

Charles II, which shows six wish–curse structures in a subjunctive total of twenty. The two twentieth-century American texts examined show the high wish—curse totals of six out of eleven and three out of thirteen, respectively. Several texts, particularly *The Three Doctors* and *Hazel Kirke,* would show even higher totals if such constructions as "Bless me", or "Confound them", had not been listed as non-distinctive subjunctives because of no subject having been stated. In such a play as *Charles II,* the wish–curse category includes the frequent formulaic reference to royalty, with the first four subjunctives listed being wishes for the royal health and prosperity (e.g., ". . . so God save the jovial king . . ." [147]).

Since in a statistically oriented study only numerical lists of structures are given, it is necessary to study the texts individually to understand the somewhat distorted and misleading patterns produced by subjunctives in such atypical categories.

A similar close inspection is necessary to understand better the development of the preterite modal inflection from its relatively unimportant position in early Modern English to its position of prominence in present-day English. Appearing infrequently in the earliest plays, with but two examples (e.g., *He wille vs marre and we were moo* [line 208]) in *Harrowing of Hell,* the construction was soon being used more frequently, accounting for seven constructions in a total of thirty-three subjunctive modal structures found in *Ralph Roister Doister,* a play that uses such comparative structures as "I will not hear him but make as I *had* haste" (line 75). In *Doctor Faustus* (1589) conditional structures are expressed by preterite forms similar to present-day ones: ". . . yet, if you *were* not dunces, you *would* never ask me. . . . (9) ; and when *The Man of Mode* (1676) was being written the auxiliaries were frequently being used in preterite structures: ". . . *should* she see you, . . . she *would* look . . ." (439). As early as *The Conscious Lovers* (1722) the modal preterite inflection *was* appears, used in the comparative structure: "You talk as if the World *was* now, just as it was when my old master and you were in your youth" (line 212). The increasing frequency of the construction is strikingly illustrated by the contemporary drama *A Taste of Honey,* in which *all* of the subjunctive structures are modal preterite inflections, typified by the conditional construction: "I said what *would* you say if I *got* a job" (13), and the noun clause after verbs of saying, thinking, wishing, commanding, etc.: "I thought you said you *weren't* good at anything" (14).

In addition to considering general linguistic and non-linguistic influences on the subjunctive patterns in dramatic textual material, it is necessary in tracing subjunctive patterns to consider specific internal linguistic influences revealed in textual evidence, specifically alternation in identical structures, atypical structures, and ambiguous structures. Some examples of such evidence, subdivided into various categories, are as follows:

1. *Alternation in Structures within a Text.* It is primarily the earliest plays which show inconsistency in expressing the subjunctive, e.g., *Noah,* in which final–*e* is sometimes omitted, as in the second verb in the following:

Saue from velany and bryng to Thi hall
And kepe me from syn . . . (line 68).

(The verbs in this construction were designated non-distinctive subjunctive forms because of uncertainty as to whether they express the subjunctive or imperative mood.)

Variation in identical subjunctive structures is also shown in *Gorboduc* in the indicative–subjunctive alternation in the compound concessive structure, "Although my brother *hath bereft* my realm,/And *bear,* perhaps, to me an hateful mind . . ." (line 172).

2. *Atypical Structures.* (a) *Curses and Wishes:* Among the atypical structures evident in several of the texts are the numerous curses and wishes discussed above. Particularly difficult to classify were verbs in the speech of Noah to God, such as the two quoted: *"Saue from velany and bryng to Thi hall . . .",* since in form *Saue* and *bryng* may be either imperative or subjunctive. Following the classification method adopted in Chapter IV (in which the verbs used by a patriarch to address a deity were also ambiguous), the two forms were classified as non-distinctive subjunctives, Category 1 (wish–curse). In addition to seeming imperative in tone, the construction presents a syntactic contrast with the following structure from the same text, which was classified as a subjunctive, Category 1: *"Now blissid be He . . ."* (line 467).

(b) *Formulaic type subjunctives:* Among the formulaic type subjunctives noted were the following constructions, all classified under the wish–curse category:

God spede, dere wife, . . . (*Noah,* line 190)
(God keep thee, worshipful Master . . .)
And *fare* well the lusty Master . . . (*Ralph Roister Doister,* line 79)
Physic, *farewell* . . . (*Doctor Faustus,* p. 4)
                                   [non-distinctive]
Sir Proteus, *save* you (*Two Gentlemen of Verona,* line 70)
                                   [non-distinctive]

(c) *Polite Category Subjunctives:* Unique to the dramatic texts was the use of what has in this research been termed the *polite* subjunctive (see **Appendix A**), the phrasing of a command or request with a past tense form of the auxiliary in order to make the expression seem less harsh or imperious. The examples below were classified as modal preterite inflections:

Oh, yes, if *ye'd care* to take it. (*Hazel Kirke,* 444)
If you *wouldn't* mind. (*The Sacred Flame,* 230)

(d) *Unusual Constructions:* Among the unusual structures classed as subjunctives was the following conditional clause from *Ralph Roister Doister,* which illustrates the early Modern English use of *and* with the meaning *if:*

But and she *knew* my mind, . . . (line 235)
[modal preterite inflection]

An interesting example of the modal preterite inflection in modern colloquial speech is this comparative subjunctive structure in *The Hairy Ape:* "Act like yuh *liked* it, yuh better—or croak yourself" (822). Other atypical constructions in *The Hairy Ape,* as mentioned above, include several subjunctive structures that were classed as non-distinctive because they represent the speech of non-native speakers of English and cannot, therefore, be presumed to reflect standard usage. An example is the following noun clause after a verb of saying, thinking, wishing, commanding, etc., which uses an inflected subjunctive but is quite obviously not delivered by a native speaker:

Py Yesus, I vish somepody *take* my first vatch for me! (820)

Among the other atypical structures (not designated as subjunctives) are these examples of what Jespersen called the archaic indicative *be:*

Gridirons, what *be* they? (*Doctor Faustus,* p. 15)
Nay, there *be* murmurs . . . (*Harold,* p. 14)
Aye, girl, times *be* hard . . . (*Hazel Kirke,* p. 439)

Also classed as indicative were eighteenth- and nineteenth-century uses of the verb form *don't* for the third person singular, present tense, as in this charming line from *The London Merchant:* "Her Disorder is so great she *don't* perceive she has laid her hand on mine" (line 132, p. 646) . Nor were such variations from standard usage as the following (from *She Stoops to Conquer*) classed as subjunctives:

When he comes to be a little stronger, who *know* what
    a year or two's Latin may do for him . . . (p. 506)

Zero forms of the subjunctive, such as the expression: ". . . a vengeance on them", in *Doctor Faustus* (p. 15) , were also excluded from the study, since the verbless constructions do not indicate formal inflection.

3. *Ambiguous Structures.* Ambiguous constructions found in the dramatic textual material fall into three major divisions: (1) atypical spellings, (2) ambiguous modal auxiliary constructions, and (3) subjunctive structures placed in the *ad hoc* syntactic category (14). Typical of the first division are the forms in *Noah* already mentioned (as variations in structure within a text) that omit *–e* and that make it necessary to classify as non-distinctive subjunctives such forms as the following:

Bot if God *help* amang, . . . (line 247)
God *send* the onys thi fill!   (line 207)

Ambiguous modal structures included such uses of *shall* as the following (in *Harrowing of Hell*), which was classed as non-distinctive—despite the fact that it apparently fits the substitution pattern ("I hope . . . soon cease our sorrows") —since the temporal idea of *shall* seems to be required for the meaning of the construction:

> Wherfore I hope oure helpe is nere,
> And sone *schall sesse* oure sorowes sadde. (line 43)

In the following conditional clause from *The Conscious Lovers,* the use of *will* is required for meaning; hence the structure was designated as non-subjunctive:

> (. . . if you doubt the Sincerity of my Love,) you *will* allow me true to my interest. (Act 1, Scene 1, line 451)

Patterning after a distinction of forms argued by Fries,[5] the form *let's* (also *lets*) was considered as a modal auxiliary construction (command category), as in the expression in *Charles II:* ". . . let's change the subject . . ." (151), while the non-contracted form *let* was considered as non-subjunctive, e.g.: "Let us talk of something else . . ." (*Charles II,* 147).

Lumped together in the *ad hoc* category were a number of vagrant expressions such as those listed below, all of which seem to indicate a conjectural or conditional type subjunctive:

> Feste! þat *were* a foule reasoune, (*Harrowing of Hell,* line 337)
> Ask my fellow if I *be* a thief . . . (*Doctor Faustus,* p. 9)
> . . . a man *were* as good have as many English counters. (*Doctor Faustus,* p. 15)
> It *were* a shame to call her back again. (*Two Gentlemen of Verona,* Act 1, Scene 2, line 51)
> . . . *'twere* best pound you. (*Two Gentlemen of Verona,* Act 1, Scene 1, line 100)

In summary, a survey of representative dramatic works

written over a period of more than five hundred years reveals certain patterns of usage, as follows:

1. Like the comparable diachronic analysis of biblical translations, the survey of dramatic works shows a marked decline in total subjunctive modal structures, varied only by a slight increase in usage late in the nineteenth century. On the evidence of these texts, inflected subjunctive forms decline to the point of non-existence in present-day English.

2. A parallel development, unique to the dramatic textual material, has been an increasing incidence of modal preterite inflections. From mid-seventeenth century to mid-nineteenth century, this construction accounted for more than 50 per cent of all subjunctive structures in British dramatic texts and exhibited a comparably high percentage in some American texts. After a brief decline late in the nineteenth century, the modal preterite inflection showed a marked increase in usage, particularly in British English, so that this structure accounts for 80 per cent and 100 per cent, respectively, of all subjunctive structures used in the two twentieth-century British texts investigated.

3. Patterns of subjunctive usage peculiar to dramatic texts include variation according to dialect and to literary genre and subject matter. Beginning early in the nineteenth century, American dramatic works have shown higher percentages of usage than the British of subjunctive modal structures and inflected subjunctives. With two exceptions, American texts show a lower percentage of modal preterite inflections per total modal structures than do comparable British texts. Variations according to literary genre indicate a higher incidence of subjunctive usage in tragedies (formal language) than in comedies

(colloquial language). Stylistic variation in modern drama is shown by a remarkably low percentage of subjunctive usage in modern plays that reflect colloquial and idiomatic patterns of speech, in contrast with the formal speech reflected in earlier tragic drama.

4. Among the dramatic texts there is a certain consistency of usage—indicated by the statistical data—in the syntactic categories of (a) wish–curse, (b) noun clauses after verbs of saying, thinking, wishing, commanding, etc., and (c) conditional statements. Uniquely, the dramatic works show a high percentage of usage of wishes and curses. In certain texts, the use of the wish–curse type subjunctives is so variable and so extreme that it tends to distort the over-all subjunctive pattern.

5. Internal linguistic influences, as illustrated by textual evidence, show a marked increase in usage of preterite modal inflections, a high percentage of formulaic constructions in dramatic texts, and the influence of colloquial and idiomatic speech on subjunctive expressions.

6. Except in the statistics for the two earliest texts, the percentages of non-distinctive forms show no consistent or significant patterns. The high percentages of such forms in the early texts confirm a pattern noted previously, i.e.: direct correlation between the frequency of non-distinctive forms and the decay of inflectional endings. Variation in percentage of non-distinctive forms in Modern English texts appears to be more directly related to syntactic category of the subjunctive, e.g.: the high percentage of wish–curse structures in which the subject of the construction is omitted, making it necessary to designate the structure as non-distinctive.

Methodological Notes

In order to obtain a body of evidence large enough to be representative of the texts (and therefore of the period and dialect represented) yet small enough to be collected and analyzed, arbitrary limits were set on the amount of textual material examined, the limit varying somewhat according to the textual category. Since it had been previously determined that the ratio of usage of subjunctive forms and structures of modality per total of finite-verb structures would offer the only practicable method of determining comparative rates of decline, textual sampling was regulated according to finite-verb count. For example: In the collecting of biblical evidence it was found that a sample containing roughly a thousand finite verbs showed sub-totals of subjunctive forms and structures of modality ranging from ninety in the Vulgate to sixteen in the American translation. Regulating sampling according to the Latin text, a count was made of all finite-verb forms in the identical material in the other five translations and all subjunctive forms and structures of modality were recorded and tabulated separately. The same technique was followed in the sampling of Old and Middle English secular writings and translations, with the total number of finite verbs varying from approximately fifteen hundred for the *Anglo–Saxon Chronicle* to five hundred (plus the respective numbers of subjunctives and structures of modality) for the literary selections and the plays. By limiting to five hundred the number of finite verbs in the indicative or imperative mood, a comparison could easily be made by contrasting with the five hundred count the total number of subjunctives and structures of modality contained in the material required to select the imperative–indicative verb forms. Tables could then be tabulated for each textual category, showing the approximate percentages of subjunctives and structures of modality. In computing percentages, a total of 500 was used as divisor except in the statistics for the biblical texts, the *Anglo-Saxon Chronicle,* and the *Harrowing of Hell.* Non-distinctive subjunctive forms were included in totals of modal constructions *only* in determining the relative percentage of non-distinctive forms per total subjunctive modal structures.

Methods of selecting textual samples were held constant within the various categories. For the biblical translations Chapters 7–14 of the Gospel of St. Matthew were used. For all other Old and Middle English texts (with the exceptions in the *Anglo–Saxon Chronicle,* the *Cursor Mundi,* and other Middle English texts noted in the appropriate chapters), the material investigated was taken from the beginning of the text or beginning of a specific division. Formal introductions or prologues were not included. In the investigation of dramatic works, samplings were always from the opening dialogue, omitting prologues and stage directions.

CLASSIFICATION OF SUBJUNCTIVES AND STRUCTURES OF MODALITY

The selection of subjunctives in the textual material was made upon the basis of formal inflectional and syntactical contrasts. Unambiguous inflected subjunctive forms, as described in grammatical studies of the respective periods,[1] were classified as *subjunctive* and were recorded and tabulated without further notation. Ambiguous forms were classified and tabulated according to criteria that varied somewhat according to historical period, dialect, or both. For example:

1. In Old English the first person singular present tense form and the second person singular preterite tense form of strong verbs were identical in the indicative and subjunctive moods. This was also true of the first person singular present tense and first and third person singular preterite tense of weak verbs. Other such formal similarities existed in the present and preterite tenses of the verbs *beon, wesan,* and *willan.* In addition, as Bloomfield observed, a number of texts show subjunctive plurals without *–n* in other than the antepronominal uses (such as *binde we, ge*), a usage that Wood had noted earlier and described as stemming from the old first person dual forms.[2]

With the exception of plural forms without final *–n,* the forms mentioned (though all labeled subjunctives in grammars and textual studies), showed no formal contrast. If these *–n*-minus plurals could be established as subjunctive by syntactical comparison with unambiguous subjunctive forms, they were classified and tabulated as subjunctives, since they did meet the criteria of formal contrast. Since it was desirable to keep a record of the Old and Middle English "subjunctive" forms that do not show formal contrast, they were also subjected to syntactical comparison with unambiguous subjunctive forms. If it was possible to establish a form as subjunctive by syntactical comparison, it was classified and tabulated as a non-distinctive subjunctive form; if it was not possible, the form in question was excluded from the study.

2. In late Old English, as A. H. Marckwardt observed,[3] the plural subjunctive in both present and preterite tenses ends in *–on* and *–an,* as well as *–en,* while the indicative plural, preterite tense, ends in *–an, –en,* or even *–e,* as well as the formerly regular *–on* ending.

Again, if it was possible to establish such ambiguous verb

forms as subjunctive by syntactical comparison, they were classified and tabulated as non-distinctive forms. On the other hand, verb forms ending in –en in syntactic structures in which an indicative form regularly occurred were compared with unambiguous indicative forms and, if so established as indicative, they were classified and tabulated as such but not indicated in tabulation of data (as are non-distinctive subjunctive forms and structures of modality). However, they were recorded and listed with the textual evidence.

3. In Middle English, as indicated in grammars and in David Reed's study of inflectional –n forms before 1500,[4] there was a much more general falling together of inflectional endings, to such an extent in some dialects that it is difficult to prove that a subjunctive paradigm existed.

Reed found that (1) in the Northern texts, all subjunctive forms were n–less, as were all indicative forms both before or after personal subject pronouns; (2) in the Central dialects after 1200, both present indicative and present subjunctive forms showed n or n–less endings, with only n–less forms before we or ge; (3) a formal contrast for mood, using n and n–less forms in both subjunctive syntactic positions and in indicative syntactic positions before we or ge and in the form syndon (but using the older indicative forms [þ, ð, d, t, and th] in other indicative structures) is shown regularly only in the Southern dialects.[5] Moreover, as Joseph and E. M. Wright noted in their Middle English grammar, both subjunctive and indicative preterite plural forms ended in –en and were, therefore, regularly non-distinctive.[6] Therefore, in classifying evidence from Middle English texts, dialectal and textual studies as well as grammars were utilized, and the inflectional criteria relative to each dialect (or, in some instances, each text) were recorded with the statistical reports. In general, it proved to be possible to classify only singular verb forms as unambiguous subjunctives, since the loss of final –n made most plural subjunctive forms non-distinctive. If ambiguous plural forms fit a syntactic pattern of comparison, they were classified and tabulated as non-distinctive subjunctive forms.

4. In Modern English and present-day English, subjunctive paradigms can no longer be said to exist. Modern English shows formal modal contrast only in the second and third person singular present tense (with some exceptions in the second person singular preterite tense, e.g., *calledst/call(e)d* but also *cast/cast* [Sweet],[7] and in the anomalous verb *be*). Present-day English, as noted in the Introduction, shows formal contrast only in the third person singular present tense form and in some forms of the verb *be*. Therefore, in selecting and classifying subjunctive forms from texts in these periods, only verb forms in the categories described were considered as subjunctive; and ambiguous forms were not regularly classified or tabulated (as non-distinctive) for either period, the arguments of Sweet and Jespersen for some identical indicative–subjunctive forms notwithstanding.[8]

5. In the classification in Modern and present-day English texts of such formulaic–type subjunctives as *please,* verbs used in stage directions, and verbs used in curses and blessings, syntactic criteria were used. For example:

(a) *Please,* discussed as a subjunctive form by Jespersen and Kennedy,[9] was classified as a subjunctive form only when used in a syntactic structure in which the formal contrast of inflection was shown, e. g., "If it please me, madam, what then?" (*The Two Gentlemen of Verona,* Act 2, Scene 1, line 121).[10]

(b) Stage directions, discussed as subjunctive forms by Jespersen,[11] were not considered in the study, since the textual sampling in dramatic works was limited to dialogue.

(c) Curses and blessings, considered subjunctives by Jespersen[12] and so classified in the present research (see Category 1, below) were classified as subjunctives with no further notation when the subject or agent invoked in the curse was named: e.g., "God *damn* yuh!" (*The Hairy Ape,* p. 826).[13] When no subject was named, the form was listed as non-distinctive, e. g., "Pass back that bottle, damn you!" (*The Hairy Ape,* p. 819).[14]

MODAL AUXILIARY CONSTRUCTIONS

Scholarly opinion on the modal use of certain auxiliaries and on the terminology for such modal structures shows, as might be expected, far greater diversity than does the recorded opinion on inflected subjunctive structures. The extremes range from the proposal of a die-hard classicist that *should* and *would* be considered as future tense forms of the subjunctive (in order to complete "the cycle of the tense forms in that mood" and thus facilitate comparison with Latin),[15] to Fries' strict refusal to term such auxiliaries or "function words" as substitutes or equivalents[16]—though Fries' comments on the matter, in his study of the functions of periphrastic *shall* and *will,* are among the most enlightening on an obscure topic.[17] Medial positions were taken by earlier grammarians (Curme and Poutsma among them), who referred to modal auxiliary constructions as substitutes. Behre (in his *Meditative–Polemic SHOULD in Modern English THAT–Clauses,* 1955), after pointing out accurately the dangers of such confusing terminology as subjunctive equivalent in a language that no longer has a subjunctive, surprisingly suggests the term "modern subjunctive" for such forms as *let . . . come, may . . . come.*[18] Descriptions of modal auxiliary constructions phrased in terminology more exact as to linguistic function are given in the handbooks of Zandvoort and Sledd.[19] Their descriptions of modal structures as developments in the language used to express modal ideas, not to replace or serve as substitutes for subjunctives, are consistent with the interpretation accepted in this investigation, and from Sledd's definition the terminology "modal auxiliary construction" was adapted.

The classification of modal auxiliary constructions demanded, however, further criteria than acceptable terminology. Obviously, as numerous studies point out, the verb forms traditionally called "auxiliaries" (*have, be, shall, will, may, should, would, can, must, ought, need,* and a few others) have functions other than expressing modality that do not fall within the scope of the present work. In classifying structures as modal auxiliary constructions, the rule of Poutsma was used— i. e., the modal auxiliary structure could be replaced by an inflected subjunctive. In applying this pattern of substitution it was necessary to apply certain additional criteria, namely diachronic considerations. In present-day usage, even on what certain grammarians term the "literary level", inflected subjunctives used in other then stereotyped expressions ("God *help* you!")[20] sound peculiar to most native speakers. Therefore, when using a pattern of substitution to determine if an auxiliary construction could be replaced by an inflected subjunctive—when subjunctives are no longer common to present-day speech—it was sometimes helpful to compare the structure with earlier usage as well. Thus the auxiliary construction in the wish—statement "That a great wave wid [with] sun in the heart of it *may sweep* me over the side . . ."[21] was classified as a modal auxiliary construction because the usage of a subjunctive was frequent in such a structure in Modern English ("Jove end me first!"[22]), and similar to present-day subjunctive usage in stereotyped expressions.[23]

The more difficult decision not to classify "will provide", in the sentence from *The Hairy Ape:* "I hope Whitechapel will provide the needed tonic", as a modal auxiliary construction was made since the substitute pattern: "I hope Whitechapel provide the needed tonic", does not compare even with earlier usage patterns. The verb *hope,* as C. H. Haile states, ". . . is commonly followed by *may* or the future indicative, rarely by modal *shall: It is hoped that the plan may [will, shall] be followed".*[24] In contrast, Haile points to the use of subjunctive or modal auxiliary constructions after such verbs as *desire* or *request* used to express desire, fear, command, etc.

("He desires [requests; it is desirable that] this be [shall, should, may, might be] done"). Therefore, *may serve* in the sentence *"I trust the kingly touch . . . / May serve to charm the tiger out of him"* (*Harold*, p. 14), was classified as a modal auxiliary construction because the verb *trust* (like *desire* and *request*) is a verb of "saying, thinking, wishing, commanding, etc.", as described under Subjunctive Category 4 below. In addition, Jespersen,[25] discussing the use of a subjunctive after such verbs, lists the example from the earlier English of Thomas More: "I thynk he be [indic?] some of the Ambassadours fooles". Since classification according to a substitution pattern that is no longer a regular usage must at times necessarily be somewhat arbitrary, such debatable classifications as those made by a substitution similar to the *may serve/serve* pattern are noted in the discussion of statistics.

In classifying auxiliaries in syntactic structures in which present-day English would show an ambiguous or non-distinctive subjunctive form in the substitute frame, e. g., "They didn't seem a bit anxious that I should investigate",[26] the structure was compared with unambiguous subjunctive forms or contrasted with a substitute pattern using an unambiguous form, e. g., *that he should investigate/that he investigate.* When established as modal by such a comparison, the structure was classified and tabulated as a modal auxiliary construction. Such modal auxiliary constructions used in first and second person singular verb forms in Modern and present-day English were indicated in the study, even though non-distinctive subjunctive forms for the periods were not, since the former structures show a syntactic contrast with the indicative mood, e. g., *that I investigate/that I should investigate.*

In most instances the use of a pattern of substitution of an inflected subjunctive facilitated the determination of non-modal usage of the auxiliary as in the text and the translation of a structure from *Melibee:* "Warre . . . hath so greet an entryng . . . that every wight *may enter* . . .", "War . . . has so high an entrance . . . every man *may enter*. . . ." [27] The substitution of the inflected subjunctive form *enter* gives a completely different meaning to the passage, so the structure was not classed as a modal auxiliary construction. So also *would* in the biblical translation "We would see a sign from thee" (King James, Matt. 12:38) was not classified as a modal auxiliary construction since the meaning of *would* as *want to* or *wish to* is revealed by substituting the non-distinctive form *see*, as well as by a comparison with the Latin and Old English translations *(volumus a te signum videre; we willaþ from þe tacen geseon)*.

Preterite forms of the auxiliaries used in constructions to indicate modal rather than temporal relationships (e. g., ". . . Whom *would* she yet *forsake*, yet *yield* him up . . . She *might preserve* us all." [28]) were classified as modal preterite inflections and are discussed below.

CLASSIFICATION OF MODAL PRETERITE INFLECTIONS

Like the modal auxiliary constructions, preterite verb forms used to show a contrast not of time but of non-fact or modification of fact versus fact have been and remain a topic of linguistic contention as to description and terminology. Kennedy, usually reasonably careful with terminology, refers to preterite forms used to indicate possible actions in present or future time as subjunctives,[29] as does Curme, who calls the non-distinctive form *struck* in "If he struck me, I would strike him", a "past subjunctive pointing to the future".[30] Jespersen, who labels such preterite forms "imaginative tense forms",[31] gives a history of the development of this usage of the modal preterite in English (quoted in part in note 31), and Behre points to the somewhat similar use of preterite indicative forms to express unreality in Old Armenian and Attic Greek.[32] Zandvoort, quoted elsewhere, describes the importance of the modal preterite inflection in present-day English and it is from his description that the term "modal preterite inflection" was adopted and adapted.

All of the above-named scholars discuss the use of preterite forms to indicate unreality or improbability; Jespersen writes of the number of structural choices available in English as follows:

> If we are talking of some future event, the choice of present or preterit denotes a slight difference only in degree of probability: if he comes to-morrow, we will tell him everything: if he came to-morrow we would tell him everything (with the variants *if he should come* and *if he were to come*—three nuances of probability) . If, on the other hand, we are talking of something in the present time, the imaginative preterit excludes the possibility: if he were in town, he would call— implying that he is not in town. Cf. on the other hand, 'If he is in town, he will call,' where the possibility is left open.[33]

Another good explanation of the shades of meaning expressed by contrasts of indicative—subjunctive and modal preterite inflections is given by Britta Marian Charleston (*Studies on the Syntax of the English Verb,* 1941) who quotes A. Darby as follows:

> If he *has* money enough *(which I am ready to believe)* he will pay you. (Accepted [condition])
> If he *have* money enough *(which I am inclined to doubt)* he will pay you. (Neutral [condition])
> If he *had* money enough *(but I know he has not)* he would pay you. (Rejected [condition]) [34]

In classifying modal preterite inflections in this study, syntactic criteria were used both to establish that the contrast was one of modality and also to determine if the modal preterite inflection appeared in a structure which required indication of non-fact or modification of fact. For example: the sentence, ". . . what *would* you say if I *got* a job . . ." [35] shows the syntactic contrasts of preterite forms *(would* and *got)* used to refer to a hypothetical future event rather than a past event; the hypotactic construction *(. . . if I got a job)* indicates a contrast of non-fact or modification of fact.

Structures in which the preterite form of an auxiliary verb was used to indicate modality (rather than to maintain sequence of tenses) were classified and tabulated as modal preterite inflections, as in the example above of *would* in the apodosis of the conditional–type sentence, or in the verb forms italicized in the following sentence: "Whom *would* she yet *forsake,* yet *yield* him up. . . . She *might preserve* us all",[36] in which the modal idea is indicated by syntactic contrasts in word order as well as by preterite modal inflections. Uniformly, *were* when used with first or third person forms was classified "subjunctive," while *was* was classified as a modal preterite inflection. (See Note 31.)

CLASSIFICATION OF NON-MODAL GRAMMATICAL STRUCTURES IN TRANSLATIONS

In classifying non-modal grammatical structures that were used in translations in rendering subjunctive forms and which, therefore, occurred in syntactic structures either identical or markedly similar to those in which a subjunctive or structure of modality was used in the original text, grammatical descriptions and terminology as given by Sledd in *A Short Introduction to English Grammar* were used. For example, a formulaic biblical expression as translated in the Latin and the five English versions was classified as follows:

Vulgate: *. . . ut adinpleretur quod dictum erat . . .*
[subjunctive]
Rushworth: *. . . þaet gefylled were . . .* [subjunctive]
Wycliffe: *. . . That it shulde be fulfilled . . .* [modal auxiliary construction]
Tyndale: *. . . To fulfill . . .* [infinitive]
King James: *. . . That it might be fulfilled . . .* [modal auxiliary construction]

Goodspeed: . . . *to fulfill what was said* . . .   [infinitive]
   (Matt. 13:35)

The text and the translation for concessive structure in *Mel-ibee* were classified as follows:

. . . al *be* it so that she perilously *be* wounded . . . [subjunctive;
                                                            subjunctive]
. . . *although* she *is* perilously wounded . . . [subordinating
                                         conjunction; indicative mood]

CLASSIFICATION OF TEXTUAL EMENDATIONS AND ATYPICAL FORMS AND STRUCTURES

In classifying subjunctives and structures of modality from the various texts, the following procedures were used in classifying forms in textual emendations and forms that were atypical:

1. *Textual emendations:* Subjunctives and structures of modality that were found in textual emendations were considered non-distinctive forms when the syntactical pattern in which the form appeared was complete enough and clear enough to warrant the conjecture of the modal form. If the structure was not complete enough to allow syntactical comparison, the form was not considered in the study. In the passage in *Havelok,* for example,

> He wrungen hondes, and wepen sore,
> And yerne preyden Cristes ore,
> þat he [wolde] turnen him
> Ut of þat yuel þat was so grim! [37]

the structure *wolde turnen* was classified as a non-distinctive modal auxiliary construction because the syntactic structure in which it appears (noun clause following verbs of wishing, commanding, desiring, etc.) regularly shows subjunctive forms or structures of modality in *Havelok,* e. g., "And preide, he *shulde yeme* hire wel".[38]

2. *Stylistic and poetic devices:* In certain of the poetic texts analyzed, variations in the spelling and form of some verbs seemed to be directly related to rime or meter, an occurrence which G. Forsström notes as frequent in late Old English and Middle English.[39] In *Havelok,* for example, the preterite form of the strong verb *bifalle* appears as *bifelle* in a structure that regularly shows an indicative form ("Say we nou forth *in* ure spelle! / In þat time, so it bifelle . . ." [40]), and the *e* is obviously added to match the final *–e* of *spelle* in the preceding line. Normally, in *Havelok,* the past tense spelling of the indicative form is *bifel,* e. g., "Bifel it so, a [ful] strong dere. . . ." [41] Such forms, if established as indicative by syntactical comparison, were classified as non-subjunctive and not tabulated in the statistics.

In other texts, particularly in nineteenth-century dramatic works, the form *be* appears in syntactic structures that regularly use an indicative form, e. g., ". . . this *be* the mill ye're asking after".[42] Such constructions are noted by both Charleston and Jespersen,[43] who consider them "archaic" or "stylistic". Such forms were classified as non-subjunctive and were not tabulated in the statistical evidence.

The Use of Meaning in Designating Modal Structures and Classifying Subjunctives According to Syntactic Category

When using a process of substitution in grammatical analysis it is necessary, as Fries points out, to control certain aspects of meaning.[44] Whenever possible, therefore, patterns of either formal or syntactic contrast were used in identifying and classifying subjunctives and structures of modality. In many instances, however, it was necessary to establish the modal designation by using the patterns of substitution with unambiguous structures described above. It was also frequently necessary to use a pattern of syntactic comparison in classifying subjunctives and structures of modality as to syntactic category.

CATEGORIES OF SUBJUNCTIVES AND STRUCTURES OF MODALITY

In tracing and interpreting the pattern of the subjunctive in English it is advantageous, if not obligatory, to have a system of classification of the forms and structures involved. Various systems of classification are to be found in the grammatical studies mentioned above. Curme used a dual system of "optative" and "potential", with subdivisions of each. Jespersen designates subjunctive forms by syntactic category: *conditional clauses, wish, temporal clauses,* etc. Zandvoort lists *wish, possibility* (potential) and *irreality* or *irrealis* as the concepts shown by the subjunctive. Behre, in his excellent monograph *The Subjunctive in Old English Poetry* uses a very elaborate system of classification, with sixteen syntactical subcategories listed under the general divisions of the "volitional" and the "non-volitional"; he also considers separately the subjunctive uses in non-dependent and dependent clauses. With a few exceptions, most of them caused by combining two or more of the categories listed by Behre, the syntactic categories of the subjunctive designated in this study are identical with Behre's. Though the system used here was eclectically developed, it was made without the benefit of Behre's inclusive list; one category, however, was later added from Behre's list.[45]

The subjunctive categories used in this book, adopted with terminological simplifications from Sweet's *Anglo–Saxon Primer, An Old English Grammar* by Quirk and Wrenn, and *A Grammar of Late Modern English* by Poutsma, are as follows:*

*N. B. Though terminology has been simplified, i. e., *wish, result clause,* etc., the terms are used with the restricted meaning of a subjunctive or structure of modality used in a syntactic structure of the type defined here.

1. Wish-Curse—Forms used in non-dependent clauses that express a wish, hope, or curse. [In grammatical studies this category is frequently referred to as *optative*.] Example:

> . . . *ece him seo heofenlice iateward*
> . . . *may the heavenly doorkeeper make him greater* (text and trans. *Anglo–Saxon Chronicle*)

2. Command—Forms used in non-dependent clauses that express an exhortation, an appeal, a command, or advice, most of which are third person constructions in which the syntactic structure and the function of the expression are similar to imperative mood constructions. The category is frequently designated as "jussive" or "hortative". Example:

> *(seþe haebbe earan) gehernisse gehere* (Rushworth Gloss)
> *(He that hath ears to hear), let him hear.* (King James)

3. Indirect Narrative or Indirect Question—Forms used (primarily in Old English) in dependent clauses that report indirect discourse or indirect questions. Example:

> & *he him aðas swor* & *gislas sealde. þet hit him georo wære swa hwilce dæge swa hi hit habban woldon.*
> *And he swore them oaths and gave hostages that the kingdom should be at their disposal whenever they might require it. . . .* (text and trans. *Anglo–Saxon Chronicle*)

4. Noun Clauses Type 1—Forms used in dependent noun clauses that express desires, fears, commands, and proposals, and which are generally used after verbs of saying, thinking, wishing, commanding, desiring, etc. Example:

> *ic wille þaet hit stande . . .*
> *I desire that all the freedoms . . . shall remain in force. . . .* (text and trans. *Anglo–Saxon Chronicle*)

5. Noun Clauses Type 2—Forms used in dependent noun clauses after impersonal verb constructions such as *it is necessary, it is desirable,* etc. Example:

genoh biþ leornere þætte he sie swa swa laruw his . . .
It is enough for the disciple that he be as his master . . .
(Rushworth Gloss and King James)

6. Purpose—Forms used in adverbial clauses of purpose, usually introduced by *that, so that,* or *lest;* in grammatical studies the category is often designated as *final clause.* Example:

(& *bebead heom þæt hiæ ne ge–cuðne ł ewisade hine dydun)*
and . . . *þætte gefylled wære þaet acwedan wæs þurh esaias þone witgan cweþende* . . .
(And charged them that they should not make him known:)
. . . *That it might be fulfilled which was spoken by Esaias the prophet, saying.* . . . (Rushworth Gloss and King James)

7. Result—Forms used in some adverbial clauses of result in which the result is anticipated; the usage is more common in Old English. The category is often designated as *consecutive clause.* Example:

ic wille þæt hi hit hælden swa kynelice þæt þær ne be numen of na geld . . .
I desire that they hold it so royally that neither tax nor rent be taken . . . (text and trans. *Anglo-Saxon Chronicle*)

8. Comparison—Forms used in adverbial clauses to express hypothetical comparison and generally introduced by *as if, as though,* or *as.* Example:

Her wæs se mona swilce he wære mid blode begoten.
In this year the moon was as if it were suffused with blood.
(text and trans. *Anglo–Saxon Chronicle*)

9. Concession—Forms used in adverbial clauses to express concession or to state an alternate hypothesis, generally introduced by *though, although, whether,* etc., and also indicated by inverted word order. Example:

. . . *ic bidde ealle þa ðe aefter me cumen, beon hi mine sunes, beon hi mine breðre* . . .

> *. . . and I enjoin all my successors, be they my sons, be they my brothers . . .* (text and trans. *Anglo–Saxon Chronicle*)

10. Time–Forms used in adverbial clauses of time, describing an action or state of the future or a conjectural event, and often introduced by such words as *before, until,* etc. Example:

> *. . . ærþon cume sunu monnæs*
> *. . . till the son of man be come.* (Rushworth Gloss and King James)

11. Conditional—Forms used in adverbial clauses of condition (protasis) and in non-dependent related clauses (apodosis) to express doubt, conjecture, condition contrary to fact, or quite impossible conditions. Usually, if the condition is assumed to be impossible rather than merely hypothetical, the verbs of both clauses are in the subjunctive mood. The protasis, or clause stating the condition, is introduced by such words as *if, as though, except, but, an(d),* and *suppose,* or indicated by inverted word order. Example:

> *For if it so were (that no man sholde be conseilled but oonly of hem that hadden lordshipe and maistrie of his persone,) men wolden not be conseilled so ofte.*
> *For if it were true, (then, in order that no man should ever be advised, save by those who had mastery over his person,) men could not so often be advised.* (text and trans. *Tale of Melibee*)

12. Polite Usage—Forms used occasionally in non-dependent and dependent clauses to indicate politeness or deference in expressing a request, stating a duty or obligation, or giving a command. Example:

> *Nurse, would you mind going to the kitchen . . . (The Sacred Flame)*

13. Relative Clause—Forms used in dependent relative clauses (or adjective clauses) describing a person or persons who fulfills(s) hypothetical conditions. The clause is usually

introduced by an indefinite pronoun, e. g., *all, each,* or by a
personal pronoun used to express an indefinite reference, e. g.,
he who (se þe). Example:

> . . . *ic bidde ealle þa ðe æfter me cumen* . . .
> . . . *I enjoin all my successors* . . . (text and trans. *Anglo–
> Saxon Chronicle*)

Similarities among a number of the above categories, evident
even in the defining statements, become much more obvious
when one attempts to classify systematically a large number of
subjunctive constructions. Similarities that are often so strong
as to make categorical designation ambiguous are pointed out
in the studies of Callaway, Shearin, Burnham, and others
who have concerned themselves with classifying subjunctives
according to syntactic category. Such similarities illustrate both
the interrelation of the subjunctive uses (capably described
by Behre[46]) and the fact that it is difficult to maintain scien-
tific precision when making classifications in which any degree
of meaning must be used. As a matter of convenience in tracing historical patterns, grammatical structures were classified
according to the above definitions as objectively and consistently as possible, but no claims to infallibility are made.
However, it seems doubtful that the few errors in classification
that may have been made could be of any great statistical
significance.

Textual Evidence

Inclusion of a portion of the textual evidence used in the preparation of this book is solely for the purpose of illustrating the methods of analysis, and is not for purposes of documentation.

A three-fold method of selecting data for inclusion was used: (1) Designation and classification of subjunctive structures of modality in textual evidence representing the chronological periods of the English language (Old, Middle, Modern, and present-day English) are listed throughout. (2) Representative examples are listed of non-subjunctive plural forms ending in *–en* found in the portion of the *Anglo–Saxon Chronicle* that was studied. (3) Finally, in order to illustrate the author's methods of analyzing verb forms, the designation of all finite verb structures in the first paragraph of Chaucer's *The Parson's Tale* is given.

In the section devoted to biblical material, the verb structures listed, unless otherwise identified, are from the King James version. Subjunctive structures from an earlier English translation or from the Latin translation are listed (immediately followed by textual designation in parentheses) when the equivalent structure in the King James version is a non-subjunctive. The same procedure has been followed in listing textual evidence for *The Parson's Tale:* if the original text shows no subjunctive structure, the structure from the translation is listed, followed by the abbreviation *(trans.)* in parentheses.

Designation and classification of the subjunctive structures are given in a fixed order, as follows: (a) line or page citation, (b) subjunctive structure, (c) modal designation, (d) classification of modal structure as to syntactic category.

The following abbreviations are used in citing textual evidence:

(1) Designation symbols include *S* for inflected subjunctive, *M* for modal auxiliary construction, *P* for modal preterite inflections, and *N* for non-distinctive subjunctive forms.

(2) Classification of the subjunctive structure according to syntactic category is indicated by the following numbers: 1—Wish or Curse; 2—Command; 3—Indirect Narrative or Indirect Question; 4—Noun Clauses following verbs of asking, thinking, wishing, commanding, etc.; 5—Noun Clauses following impersonal verb constructions; 6—Purpose Clauses; 7—Result Clauses; 8—Comparison Clauses; 9—Concession Clauses; 10—Time Expressions; 11—Conditional Clauses; 12—Polite Usage Expressions; 13—Relative Clauses; 14—*Ad Hoc* category.

The orthography of this Appendix preserves the spellings of the editions consulted, but diacritical markings used by some editors have been deleted.

The subjunctives are listed consecutively, in order of their appearance in the texts. Citations vary in style according to type of text and the edition used: (a) the biblical gloss and translations, by chapter and verse (e.g., St. Matthew, 7:1); (b) the *Anglo-Saxon Chronicle* and translation, by year only; (c) the Chaucer tales, by sentence; (d) dramatic texts, by line in some cases, by page in others. The single exception for a text with double columns of print is indicated.

BIBLICAL TEXTS

St. Matthew, 7:1, *be (not) judged,* S, 6. 4, *caste out* (Wy-

cliffe), N, 6. 5, *awearpe* (Rush. Gloss), S, 7. 6, *mittatis* (Rush.),
S, 6; *defoulen, tobreke* (Wycliffe), N, 6. 9, *ask,* S, 11. 10, *ask,*
S, 11. 11, *ben* (Wycliffe), N, 9. 12, *should do,* P, 4. 28,
consummasset (Rush.), S, 10.

St. *Matthew,* 8:1, *discendisset* (Rush.), S, 10. 2, *maist
make* (Wycliffe), N, 11. 4, *sæcge* (Rush. Gloss), S, 3. 5, *introisset* (Rush.), S, 10. 8, *shouldest come,* P, 7. 13, *be (it) done,*
S, 2. 14, *uenisset* (Rush.), S, 10. 17, *might be fulfilled,* M, 6.
20, *reste* (Wycliffe), S, 13. 24, *operetur* (Rush.), S, 7. 28,
posset (Rush.), 8, 7. 31, *awearpa* (Rush. Gloss), S, 11. 34,
would depart, M, 3.

St. *Matthew,* 9:2, *be forgiven,* S, 2. 4, *uidisset* (Rush.), S,
10. 5, *be forgiven,* S, 2. 6, *may know,* M, 6. 9, *transire [sic]*
(Rush.), S, 10. 12, *be,* S, 13. 13, *sie* (Rush. Gloss), S, 4. 21,
may (but) touch, N, 11; *shall be,* N, 11. 29, *be,* S, 2. 30, *know,*
S, 3. 38, *will send,* M, 4.

St. *Matthew,* 10:1, *shulde casten, shulden heele* (Wycliffe),
M, 6. 6, *perisheden* (Wycliffe), N, 13. 11, *shall enter,* M, 13.
11, *sie* (Rush. Gloss), S, 3. 11, *ut-gæn* (Rush. Gloss), S, 10.
13, *be* (Tyndale), S, 11; *shall come* (Tyndale), M, 11. 13, *be*
(Tyndale), S, 11; *shall return* (Tyndale), M, 11. 19, *shall
speak,* N, 3. 19, *shall speak,* N, 3. 23, *be come,* S, 10. 25, *be,*
S, 5. 26, *drede* (Wycliffe), N, 2. 26, *shall (not) be revealed,
shall (not) be known,* M, 13. 34, *cwome* (Rush. Gloss), N, 4.
39, *gemoete, forlease* (Rush. Gloss), S, 13.

St. *Matthew,* 11:1, *consummasset* (Rush.), S, 10. 1, *lærde,
bodade* (Rush. Gloss), N, 6. 2, *audisset* (Rush.), S, 10. 3,
should come, P, 13. 14, *was,* P, 13. 15, *hæbbe* (Rush. Gloss),
S, 13. 15, *gehere* (Rush. Gloss), N, 2. 21, *be, be* (Tyndale),
S, 1. 21, *had been done,* P, 11; *would have repented,* M, 11.
23, *had been done,* P, 11; *would have remained,* M, 11. 27,
will reveal, M, 13.

St. *Matthew,* 12:3, *didde* (Wycliffe), N, 3. 7, *had known,*
P, 11; *would (not) have condemned,* M, 11, 9, *transiset*
(Rush.), S, 10. 10, *might accuse,* M, 6. 11, *shall have,* M, 13.
11, *fall,* S, 11; *will . . . lay hold,* M, 11. 14, *might destroy,*

M, 3. 16, *should (not) make (him) known,* M, 3. 17, *might be fulfilled,* M, 6. 20, *send,* S, 10. 22, *loqueretur, uideret* (Rush.), S, 7. 23, *sie* (Rush. Gloss), S, 3. 26, *cast,* S, 11. 29, *bind,* S, 11. 46, *sprece* (Rush. Gloss), S, 3.

St. Matthew, 13:2, *sederet* (Rush.), S, 7. 9, *hæbbe* (Rush. Gloss), S, 13. 9, *gehere* (Rush. Gloss), N, 2. 14, *be fulfilled* (Wycliffe), S, 6. 15, *should see,* . . . *hear* . . . *should understand* . . . *should be converted* . . . *should heal,* P, 6. 25, *dormierent* (Rush.), S, 10. 26, *creuisset* (Rush.), S, 10. 28, *gæn, gesomnige* (Rush. Gloss), S, 4. 29, *draw* (Wycliffe), N, 6. 35, *might be fulfilled,* M, 6. 43, *hæbbe* (Rush. Gloss), S, 13. 43, *gehoære* (Rush. Gloss), N, 2. 48, *essent* (Rush.), S, 10. 53, *consummasset* (Rush.), S, 10. 54, *wondriden, seiden* (Wycliffe), N, 7.

St. Matthew, 14:7, *wolde give* (Tyndale), M, 3. 7, *wolde ask* (Tyndale), M, 13. 13, *audisset, audissent* (Rush.), S, 10. 15, *may go* . . . *buy,* M, 6. 19, *iussiset* (Rush.), S, 10. 22, *lefte* (Wycliffe), N, 10. 26, *wære,* (Rush. Gloss), S, 3. 28, *be,* S, 11. 29, *cuome* (Rush. Gloss), S, 6. 30, *coepisset* (Rush.), S, 10. 32, *ascendisset* (Rush.), S. 10. 34, *trans-fretassent* (Rush.), S, 10. 35, *cognouissent* (Rush.), S, 10. 36, *might (only) touch,* M, 3.

ANGLO-SAXON CHRONICLE

Representative examples of indicative verb forms ending in –en) 656; *bidden, senden, liggen, gewriten, ietten, lovien;* 675: *sprecan haven;* 694: *geðingoden;* 729: *atewoden;* 794: *forð-ferden;* 823: *adrifen;* 870: *fordiden* . . . *comen;* 875: *riden;* 885: *ofslogen;* 963: *hæfden (ær) tobrocon; macen, wircen, lægen;* 979: *nolden* . . . *wrecan, nolden* . . . *onbugan;* 998: *lagen.*

THE PARSON'S TALE

Modal classification of all finite verbs in the first paragraph: wole, indic.; *wole,* indic.; *comen,* subjunctive—nondist. category 4; *is,* indic.; *amonesteth,* indic.; *seith,* indic.; *Stondeth,* imper.; *seeth,* imper.; *axeth,* imper.; *is,* ind.; *is,* indic.; *walketh,* imper.; *shal fynde,* indic.; *been,* indic.; *leden,* indic.; *is,* indic.; *may* (not) *fayle,* indic.; *hath mysgoon,* indic.; *is clepid,* indic.; *sholde (gladly) herknen . . . enquere,* indic.; *is,* indic.; *is cleped,* indic.; *been,* indic.; *been,* indic.; *apertenen,* indic.; *bihoven,* indic.; *destourben,* indic.

Subjunctives and structures of modality designated in the section analyzed: Sentence: 74, *comen,* N, 3. 81, *may learn* (trans.) , M, 6. 90, *be,* S, 9. 90, *may arise,* M, 11; *have,* S, 11. 92, *(synne) forlete (hem),* S, 10. 95, *be baptized,* S, 11. 96, *be,* S, 11; *may (not) bigynne,* M, 11. 97, *be baptized,* S, 11; *have,* S, 10. 133, *shal remembre,* M, 2; *looke,* S, 2; *be,* S, 4. 143, *wiste,* P, 9; *sholde (nevere) knowe,* P, 4; *wolde* (I) *have,* P, 9. 146, *were,* S, 9. 149, *have, offend, sin* (trans.) , S, 11. 149, *sholdest do,* P, 11. 150, *be,* S, 6. 155, *were,* S, 13. 174, *shal (not) turne,* M, 4. 202, *wolden . . . eten, myghte,* P, 11. 212, *sholde dye,* P, 8. 217, *be,* S, 9. 227, *wolde (wel) understande . . . bithynke . . . sholde have,* P, 11. 228, *hadde . . . wolde make,* P, 13. 235, *returne,* S, 11; *shal (he) lyve,* M, 11. 242, *be,* S, 9; *availle,* N, 9. 244, *have,* S, 7.

DRAMATIC TEXTS

1. *Harrowing of Hell,* Line: 24, *be done,* S, 10. 26, *shulde wende,* M, 3. 43, *schall sesse,* N, 4. 65, *late,* N. 1. 95, *schalle (sone) passe,* M, 4. 109, *save,* S, 11; *schal,* M, 11. 139, *mot (þou) spede,* M, 1. 141, *calle-crie,* S, 11. 152, *passe,* S, 4. 154, *be,* N, 10. 156, *go,* S, 10. 175, *deprive,* S, 11; *will (ȝe) witte,* M, 11. 177, *be,* S, 4. 202, *shulde be boune,* M, 4. 203, *made,* P, 11. 209, *wille (vs) marre,* M, 11; *wer,* P, 11. 211, *be grathed,* S, 4. 226, *schulde passe—wonne,* M, 5. 251, *schulde noȝt (be) kidde,* M, 6. 253, *were tolde,* S, 4. 268, *begynne,* N, 14. 269, *schulde be obitte—schulde entre—saue,* M, 3. 277, *twynne,* N, 10. 305, *were,* S, 9. 327, *be,* S, 11. 331, *take,* N, 11; *be betraied,* S, 11. 336, *schalte flitte,* M, 6. 337, *were,* S, 14. 340, *flitte,* S, 6. 343, *helpe,* N, 1. 399, *drawe,* N, 6. 400, *blisse,* S, 1. 405, *be,* S, 1.

2. *Noah*, Line: 55, *will take*, M, 6. 67, *Save—kepe—here*, N, 1. 122, *be*, S, 4. 148, *be*, S, 10. 157, *be soght*, S, 4. 187, *be*, S, 11. 190, *spede*, S, 1. 191, *myght* (I) *thryfe*, M, 1. 200, *were*, P, 14. 201, *be*, S, 9. 207, *send*, N, 1. 210, *teyn*, N, 11. 218, *smyte*, S, 11; *shal turne*, M, 11. 231, *stryke*, S, 11; *will (she) skryke*, M, 11. 238, *fare*, S, 1. 243, *myght (I) thrife*, M, 1. 247, *help*, N, 11. 256, *blissid be*, S, 1. 263, *flyt*, N, 10. 296, *be*, S, 11. 300, *blissid be*, S, 1. 312, *Hy—go*, N, 2. 317, *be*, S, 6. 328, *myght (I) the*, M, 1. 333, *have*, N, 1. 339, *were*, S, 14. 361, *like*, N, 11. 386, *do*, S, 11; *shall (I) breke*, M, 11. 388, *were*, S, 11; *Might . . . haue*, P, 11. 394, *were*, P, 4. 396, *were*, S, 4. 398, *luf*, N, 11. 402, *haue (I)*, N, 1. 408, *Oute*, N, 1. 427, *Help*, N, 1. 429, *rewle*, N, 1. 454, *shuld haue*, P. 11; *were*, P. 11. 467, *blissid be*, S, 1. 486, *send*, N, 1. 488, *Pray*, N, 2. 490, *wold send*, P, 4. 494, *Thank (we)*, N, 2. 502, *fynd*, N, 11. 514, *myght (the) befall*, M, 1. 526, *were*, P, 4.

3. *Ralph Roister Doister*, Line: 6, *be*, S, 3. 10, *betide*, S, 11. 39, *smile—cast*, S, 11. 43, *take*, S, 11. 75, *had*, P, 8. 79, *keep—fare*, S, 1. 89, *help*, S, 11. 92, *be*, S, 9. 109, *be*, S, 11. 132, *save*, S, 1. 153, *be*, S, 11. 158, *were*, S, 11. 200, *had*, P, 4. 214, *be*, S, 10. 230, *were*, S, 14. 230, *should (it) break*, M, 5. 235, *knew*, P, 11; *would be—think*, M, 11. 253, *were*, S, 11. 256, *keep*, S, 11. 272, *dwell*, S, 4. 274, *stand*, S, 9. 278, *save*, S, 1. 322, *choose*, S, 9. 339, *were*, P, 14. 354, *yelde*, S, 1. 366, *might be*, P, 11; *were*, P, 11. 367, *were*, S, 14. 374, *knew*, P, 11.

4. *Gorboduc*, Line: 55, *bring*, S, 11; *shall befall*, M, 11. 69, *end*, S, 1. 100, *Shall light*, M, 6. 167, *be*, S, 14. 202, *Be brought*, S, 11. 209, *may (longer) live*, M, 6. 212, *be*, S, 10. 212, *be*, S, 4. 225, *do last*, S, 10. 242, *be*, S, 7. 320, *do agree*, S, 9. 323, *be deem'd*, S, 4. 358, *serve*, S, 11. 394, *be foreseen*, S, 6. 406, *remain*, S, 4. 421, *corrupt—writhe*, S, 6. (Act II) : 16, *adjudge*, S, 11; *conceived*, P, 11. 48, *bring*, S, 10. 73, *be*, N, 1. 81, *had pinched*, P, 11; *be*, S, 11. 97, *be deemed*, S, 6. 103, *have . . . got*, S, 10. 115, *may be*, M, 6. 117, *end, pay*, S, 11. 130, *be*, S, 9. 135, *be placed*, S, 11. 138, *turn, end*, S, 10. 172,

bear, S, 9. 191, *break,* S, 11. 197, *defend,* S, 1. 199, *Had (erst) been heard,* P, 1. 212, *help,* S, 11; *(woe unto),* N, 11.

5. *Doctor Faustus,* Page: 4, *Couldst (thou) make,* P, 11; were, S, 11. 4, *farewell,* N, 1. 6, *tempt—heap,* S, 6. 8, *cease,* S, 10. 9, *be,* S, 14. 9, *were,* P, 11; *would (never) ask,* P, 11. 9, *were,* S, 11. 10, *bless—preserve—keep,* S, 1. 10, *were,* S, 11; *should* (I) *grieve,* P, 11. 11, *be,* S, 9. 12, *will (we) come,* M, 11; *use,* S, 11. 12, *be,* S, 1. 13, *Had,* P, 11. 13, *be,* S, 8. 13, *I'd give,* P, 11. 13, *return,* S, 10. 14, *would give,* P, 11; *were,* S, 9. 14, *'twere,* S, 9. 14, *had need have,* P, 11. 14, *were,* S, 11; *should be,* P, 11. 14, *had paid,* P, 8. 15, *were,* S, 14. 15, *should kill,* P, 11; *would (folks) say,* P, 11. 15, *should serve,* P, 11; *would (you) teach,* P, 11. 16, *forgive,* S, 1. 18, *torture,* N, 14. 20, *please,* S, 13. 20, *give,* S, 1. 20, *change,* S, 10.

6. *Two Gentlemen of Verona,* Line: 3, *Were't,* S, 11; *would entreat,* P, 11. 16, *do environ,* S, 11. 46, *blow,* S, 10. 61, *bechance,* S, 1. 70, *save,* N, 1. 75, *be,* S, 11. 98, *be,* S, 11; *were,* P, 11. 100, *'twere,* S, 14. 123, *may be . . . delivered,* M, 6. (Scene 2): 7, *please,* N, 11. 11, *were,* P, 11; *should be,* N, 11. 26, *thought,* P, 11. 33, *knew,* P, 4. 46, *be,* S, 4. 51, *were,* S, 14. 67, *were,* S, 4. 79, *will (not) live,* M, 11; *have,* S, 11. 86, *were,* S, 11; *would (you) sing,* P, 11. 104, *were,* S, 4. 115, *be healed,* S, 10. (Scene 3): 5, *Would suffer,* M, 3. 24, *were,* S, 14. 29, *'Twere,* S, 14. 29, *sent,* P, 5. 35, *mayst perceive,* M, 6. 39, *may (it) please,* M, 1. 48, *would applaud,* P, 1. 52, *May't please,* M, 1. 73, *Please,* N, 11. 81, *should take,* M, 6. (Act II): 62, *had—had,* P, 1. 76, *were,* P, 4. 76, *would cease,* P, 6. 102, *stead,* S, 11; *will write,* M, 11. 103, *Please,* N, 11. 118, *Please,* N, 11. 120, *please,* S, 11. 121, *please,* S, 11. 122, *please,* S, 11.

7. *Man of Mode,* Page: 438, *had heard,* P, 4. 438, *may look,* M, 6. 439, *be,* S, 3. 439, *may breed,* M, 6. 439, *should (she) see,* P, 11; *would look,* P, 11; *had,* P, 11. 440, *(God) a (mercy),* N, 1. 441, *mend,* N, 1. 441, *should betray,* P, 11; *would make,* P, 11. 442, *Damn,* N, 1. 442, *intend,* N, 7. 443, *make,* S, 11; *I'll*

be, M, 11. 443, *damn*, N, 1. 444, *may . . . give*, M, 1. 444, *were*, S, 11; *should cry*, N, 11. 445, *had been lost*, P, 11; *had . . . bestowed*, P, 11. 445, *were*, S, 11.

8. *All For Love*, Page: 17, *Avert*, S, 1. 18, *should*, P, 5. 18, *would . . . bear*, P, 11; *were*, S, 11. 18, *be vanquished—make*, S, 11. 18, *Had*, P, 11; *should perish*, P, 11. 19, *would . . . forsake—yield*, P, 11; *might preserve*, P, 11. 19, *should approach*, M, 3. 19, *had (never) seen*, P, 4. 20, *Live, live*, S, 1. 20, *Be—repeat*, S, 2. 20, *should animate*, P, 6. 21, *had slept*, P, 4. 21, *had called*, P, 10. 21, *wouldst . . . give*, P, 14. 21, *were*, S, 8. 22, *be*, S, 4. 22, *grew*, P, 8. 23, *said*, P, 11; *'twere*, S, 11. 26, *wert*, P, 1. 26, *had (I) been*, P, 11; *needed*, P, 11.

9. *The Conscious Lovers*, Line: 2, *should (not) be interrupted*, M, 4. 60, *had*, P, 8. 88, *had been*, P, 8. 116, *forbid*, S, 1. 123, *were*, S, 11. 197, *might learn*, M, 6. 212, *was*, P, 8. 225, *had (not) made*, P, 8. 374, *were*, S, 9. 379, *were*, S, 4. 387, *should be*, P, 5; *be*, S, 5. 437, *knew*, P, 11. (Scene 2) : 9, *should (not) refuse*, P, 11. 31, *had known—was*, P, 4. 72, *will have*, M, 11.

10. *The London Merchant*, Line: 1, *be praised*, S, 1. 26, *should be tempted*, P, 11; *may reject*, M, 11. 32, *Shou'd . . . bring*, N, 11. 88, *may . . . commend*, M, 6. 101, *would dispense*, P, 4. 107, *shou'd (you) be*, P, 11. 127, *would have been*, P, 11; *had deprived*, P, 11. 141, *should learn*, P, 6. 145, *should confirm*, P, 4. 150, *had (you) been*, P, 11; *had been*, P, 11. 155, *had (you) asserted—insisted*, P, 11; *had submitted*, P, 11. 170, *should*, P, 4. (Scene 2) : 108, *be*, S, 11. 123, *had expected*, P, 4. 139, *were*, S, 11; *should desire*, P, 11. 157, *were*, S, 11. 171, *Had (I) been*, P, 11. 200, *should (I) wrong*, P, 11; *should forgive*, P, 11. 200, *might forgive*, P, 9. 224, *will stay*, M, 11; *you'd have*, P, 11. 263, *were*, S, 11; *would . . . be*, P, 11. 276, *may prove*, M, 4. 278, *Should (she) trifle*, P, 11. (Act II) : 5, *were*, S, 8. 10, *may . . . conceal*, M, 9. 26, *were*, S. 4. 28, *knew*, P, 11. 61, *knew*, P, 8. 97, *'twill ease*, M, 11; *should (it) admit*, P, 11.

11. *She Stoops to Conquer*, Page: 506, *be*, S, 11. 507, *be*,

S, 11. 508, *Bless,* N, 1. 509, *be,* S, 11. 510, *bless,* N, 1. 510, *be,*
S, 11. 511, *were—were,* S, 4. 512, *be,* S, 9; *bees,* N, 9. 512, *May
(this) be,* M, 1. 512, *damn,* N, 1. 513, *pleased,* P, 11; *could
be revenged,* P, 11. 516, *shall want,* M, 11. 516, *bless,* N, 1. 517,
made, P, 9. 517, *should call,* P, 11; *will (you) behave,* M, 11.

12. *School for Scandal,* Page, Column and Line: 988b-43,
were, S, 4. 989a-31, *had been,* P, 11; *would (not) have been,*
M, 11. 990a–41, *would report,* P, 4. 990a–43, *had,* P, 11. 991a–
20, *should believe,* P, 4. 991b–31, *was,* P, 11; *would be,* P, 11.
992b–12, *had . . . seen,* P, 8. 993a–1, *may (not) be deceived,*
M, 4. 993a–16, *had,* P, 11.

13. *Three Doctors,* Page: 123, *Should give,* M, 6. 123, *Pless—
pless,* N, 1. 124, *may (just) sit,* M, 6. 125, *send,* S, 1. 126,
Pless—pless, N, 1. 127, *could (almost) fancy,* P, 7. 128, *should
despise,* P, 11; *could forget,* P, 11. 129, *close,* S, 9. 129, *Bless,*
N, 1. 130, *damne,* N, 1. 132, *were,* S, 11; *would knock,* P, 11.
135, *Pless—pless,* N, 1. 135, *should (never) see,* M, 4. 137, *had,*
P, 11. 139, *Will emancipate,* M, 11. *139, damn,* N, 1. 139,
I'll fight, M, 11. 141, *did,* P, 11; *should have,* P, 11. 142, *I'll
leave,* M, 11; *(will) be,* M, 11. 148, *were,* S, 9.

14. *Charles II,* Page: 147, *bless,* S, 1. 147, *help,* S, 1. 147,
save—send, S, 1. 147, *will (but) end,* M, 4. 147, *should offer,*
P, 11. 147, *were,* S, 11. 147, *should trick,* P, 11. 147, *be,* S, 9.
147, *be,* S, 1. 149, *forfend,* S, 1. 149, *should take,* P, 4. 149, *will
judge,* M, 11; *should . . . be,* P, 11. 151, *let's change,* M, 2. 151,
let's talk, M, 2. 151, *had,* P, 11. 151, *he'd teach,* P, 11. 152, *may
(not) please,* M, 4. 152, *Should . . . chance,* P, 11.

15. *Harold,* Page: 13, *may (he) tell,* M, 1. 14, *blast,* S, 11.
15, *May serve,* M, 4. 19, *pass,* S, 11. 20, *should harp,* P, 7. 20,
be, S, 11; *were,* S, 11. 22, *let go,* S, 10, 23, *went—went,* P, 4.
23, *be,* S, 11. 26, *shalt . . . be,* M, 11. 28, *be,* S, 6. 29, *were,* S,
14. 31, *were,* P, 4. 32, *take,* S, 11; *should be,* P, 11. 33, *Had
(I) been,* P, 11; *would have spoil'd,* P, 11. 33, *wert,* P, 1. 34,
shall roll, M, 10. 34, *be,* S, 11. 35, *were,* S, 11. 36, *Should
yield,* P, 6. 36, *were,* S, 14. 36, *found,* P, 11. 36, *Should not,*
P, 11; *stay,* S, 11. 36, *may do,* M, 4. 36, *may play,* M, 6. 37,

bless, N, 1. 38, *should come,* P, 4. 39, *shall have shown—redden'd,* M, 10. 41, *had swallowed,* P, 4.

15a. *The Second Mrs. Tanqueray,* Page: 782, *confound,* N, 1. 783, *wanted,* P, 13. 783, *let's face,* M, 2. 784, *Bless,* N, 1. 784, *would unman,* P, 14. 784, *enter,* S, 2. 784, *would (I) hasten,* P, 12. 784, *could carry,* P, 8. 785, *Had (she) belonged,* P, 11; *would have defined,* P, 11. 785, *would symbolize,* P, 11. 785, *would get,* P. 11. 785, *You'd (scarcely) believe,* P, 11. 785, *could prove,* P, 4. 785, *you'll excuse,* M, 11. 786, *take,* S, 1. 786, *confound,* N, 1. 786, *Bless,* N, 1. 787, *were,* S, 8. 787, *couldn't realize,* M, 8. 787, *Let's talk,* M, 2. 788, *will,* M, 11. 788, *should feel,* M, 4. 788, *were,* S, 8. 788, *intended,* P. 11. 788, *should tender,* P, 4. 788, *were,* S, 11; *should care,* P, 11. 788, *Confound,* N, 1. 789, *should like,* P, 12. 789, *might restrain,* P. 13. 790, *bless,* S, 1. 790, *Would (you) prefer,* P, 12.

16. *Hazel Kirke,* Page: 439, *be hanged,* S, 1. 439, *were,* S, 11. 439, *be,* N, 4. 440, *bless,* N, 1. 440, *Drat—drat—Confound,* N, 1. 440, *bless,* S, 1. 440, *might learn,* M, 6. 440, *may happen—may change,* M, 4. 440, *were,* S, 11; *I'd drive,* P, 11. 441, *were,* S, 5. 441, *be—keep,* S, 1. 441, *thank,* N, 1. 441, *won't go,* M, 11. 442, *were,* S, 11. 442, *were,* S, 11. 442, *were,* S, 4. 443, *was,* P, 11. 443, *I'd be,* P, 11; *didn't,* P, 11. 444, *Bless,* N, 1. 444, *would . . . say,* P, 11; *were,* S, 11. 444, *ye'd care,* P, 12. 444, *bless,* N, 1. 444, *Confound,* N, 1.

16a. *Shenandoah,* Page: 479, *would prevent,* P, 11; *could,* P, 11. 479, *would (not) dare,* P, 3. 480, *were,* S, 8. 480, *should go,* P, 11; *might go,* P, 11. 480, *had (he) lived,* P, 11. 480, *had (just) reached,* P, 8. 482, *had,* P, 4. 482, *I'd like,* P, 12. 482, *I'd like,* P, 12. 482, *Would (you) like,* P, 12. 483, *bless,* N, 1. 484 *shall (not) refuse,* N, 11. 484, *Damn,* N, 1. 484, *should learn,* P, 11; *would kill,* P, 11. 484, *should like,* P, 12. 484, *could (hardly) have,* P, 11; *had been,* P, 11. 484, *had . . . confessed,* P, 11; *could (not) have believed,* P, 11. 484, *should (not) know,* P, 4. 485, *was,* P, 8.

17. *The Sacred Flame,* Page: 226, *moved,* P, 11; *you'd make,* P, 11. 226, *were,* S, 8. 227, *would—gave—murmured,* P. 11. 228,

I'd (just) ask, P, 4; *would like,* P, 12. 229, *wouldn't mind,* P, 12. 230, *Let's send, have,* M, 2. 230, *had,* P, 5. 230, *damn,* N, 1. 232, *should know,* P, 4. 237, *knew,* P, 8. 238, *would (you) mind,* P, 12. 240, *was,* P, 8.

18. *The Hairy Ape,* Page: 819, *stiffen,* S, 1. 819, *damn,* N, 1. 819, *mend,* S, 1. 820, *take,* N, 4. 820, *help,* S, 1. 821, *take,* S, 1. 821, *have,* S, 1. 822, *may sweep,* M, 1. 822, *liked,* P, 8. 823, *Let's (just) talk,* M, 2. 824, *should investigate,* M, 6.

19. *A Taste of Honey,* Page: 7, *She'd lose,* P, 11; *was,* P, 11. 8, *you've done,* P, 11. 11, *You'd sniff,* P, 11; *had,* P, 11. 13, *would (you) say,* P, 11; *did,* P, 11; 13, *would (you) say,* P, 11; *got,* P, 11. 14, *weren't,* P, 4.

19a. *A Subject of Scandal and Concern,* Page: 16, *Would (you) mind,* P, 12. 16, *cost,* P, 11; *would be put,* P, 11. 17, *be (it) spoken,* S, 2. 18, *may appear,* M, 9. 19, *should like,* P, 12. 20, *would assure,* P, 11. 20, *Would (you) object,* P, 12. 21, *should give,* P, 4. 22, *should save,* P, 12. 23, *should fail,* P, 14. 27, *had (he) given,* P, 11; *might have been defeated,* P, 11. 28, *should place, leave,* P, 14. 29, *Would (you) have lost,* P, 11; *had (not) come,* P, 11. 29, *would have felt,* P. 4.

20. *Death of a Salesman,* Page: 1064, *I'd've gone,* P, 11; *might've killed,* P, 11. 1064, *Goddammit,* S, 1. 1064, *was,* P, 11; *I'd a been,* P. 11. 1064, *goddammit,* S, 1. 1066, *got started,* P, 11. 1067, *goddammit,* S, 1. 1067, *were,* P, 11; *I'd be,* P, 11. 1067, *were,* S, 11. 1067, *let's go,* M, 2. 1067, *Let's go,* M, 2.

20a. *Command Decision,* Page: 1156, *they'd fire,* P, 4. 1156, *would (you) like,* P, 12. 1156, *wasn't,* P, 11; *we'd . . . have,* P, 11. 1156, *they'd fight,* P, 4. 1157, *Would . . . like,* P, 12. 1157, *could have,* P, 11. 1158, *Damn,* N, 1. 1158, *I'd known,* P, 11; *should have been,* P, 11. 1159, *wouldn't like,* P, 13. 1159, *weren't,* P, 8. 1160, *Would (someone) mind,* P, 12. 1160, *I'd written,* P, 4. 1160, *should like,* P, 12. 1160, *could do,* P, 4. 1160, *Let's see,* M, 2. 1161, *had been told,* P, 4.

Notes

INTRODUCTION

1. H. W. Fowler, *A Dictionary of Modern English Usage* (Oxford: The Clarendon Press, 1926), p. 574; and *ibid.*, revised 1965, p. 595.

2. In addition to the works discussed in some detail elsewhere in this book, the following contributions are especially worthy of note: Morgan Callaway, Jr., *The Consecutive Subjunctive in Old English* (Boston: D. C. Heath & Co., 1933) and *The Temporal Subjunctive in Old English* (Austin: University of Texas, 1931); H. F. Field, "Comparative Syntax and Some Modern Theories of the Subjunctive", *Modern Philology*, XXIII (1925), 201–224; Randolph Quirk, *The Concessive Relation in Old English Poetry* (New Haven: Yale Press, 1954); and George W. Cobb, "The Subjunctive Mood in Old English Poetry", *Philologica: The Malone Anniversary Studies* (Baltimore: Johns Hopkins Press, 1950), R. W. Zandvoort ("On the So-Called Subjunctive", *English Language Teaching*, XVII [January, 1963]) refers to a number of recent articles and handbook summaries on the topic, as does W. H. Hirtle ("The English Present Subjunctive", *Canadian Journal of Linguistics*, IX [1964]).

3. Both definitions and terminology are adapted from the descriptions of mood, modal auxiliaries, modal preterites, and the subjunctive mood that appear in James H. Sledd, *A Short Introduction to English Grammar* (Chicago: Scott, Foresman & Co., 1959), and R. W. Zandvoort, *A Handbook of English Grammar* (7th ed.; Groningen: J. B. Wolters, 1959). The example sentences for the definition of "subjunctive mood" are from Sledd, p. 219, and Zandvoort, pp. 104, 258, 105.

4. Hendrik Poutsma, *Mood and Tense of the English Verb* (Groningen: P. Noordhoff, 1922), p. 2.

5. Example sentence from Zandvoort, *A Handbook of English Grammar*, p. 81.

6. *Ibid.*, pp. 74, 76.

7. Hans-Oskar Wilde, "Aufforderung, Wunsch und Möglichkeit", *Anglia*, LXIII (1939), Teil I, 247; Etsko Kruisinga, *A Handbook of Present-Day English* (5th ed.; Groningen: P. Noordhoff, 1932), III, 527–529.

CHAPTER ONE

1. A. G. Kennedy, *Current English* (Boston: Ginn & Co., 1935), p. 464.

2. Catherine M. Nesbitt, "The Whim of the Moment", *Die Neueren Sprachen,* No. 5 (1961), pp. 238–244.

3. W. H. Hirtle, *op. cit.,* pp. 75–82.

4. W. M. Ryan, "More on Pseudo-Subjunctive 'Were'", *American Speech,* XXXVII (1962), pp. 114–122.

5. R. W. Zandvoort, "On the So-Called Subjunctive", pp. 73–77.

6. E. L. Hettich and A. G. C. Maitland, *Latin Fundamentals* (3rd ed.; Englewood Cliffs: Prentice–Hall, Inc., 1958), p. 178; Wilde, *op. cit.,* Teil I, 211ff. and Teil III, 97.

7. G. O. Curme and Hans Kurath, *A Grammar of the English Language* (Boston: D. C. Heath & Co., 1931–35), III, 390; Zandvoort, *A Handbook of English Grammar,* p. 382.

8. J. R. Kantor, *An Objective Psychology of Grammar* (Bloomington: Indiana University Press, 1952), pp. 278–290.

9. Britta Marian Charleston, *Studies on the Syntax of the English Verb* (Bern: A. Francke A.G., 1941), pp. 194–202.

10. Goold Brown, *The Grammar of English Grammars* (New York: W. Wood, 1862), pp. 337–338.

11. Zandvoort, "On the So-Called Subjunctive", p. 78.

12. Otto Jespersen, *The Philosophy of Grammar* (London: G. Allen & Unwin, 1924), pp. 317–318.

13. Otto Jespersen, *A Modern English Grammar on Historical Principles* [hereafter *A Modern English Grammar*] (London: G. Allen & Unwin, 1954), Parts II–VII.

14. H. Poutsma, *A Grammar of Late Modern English* (5 vols.; Groningen: P. Noordhoff, 1926), Part II, Sec. II, pp. 13, 161–202.

15. Curme, *op. cit.*, pp. x, 393–394.

16. C. C. Fries, *American English Grammar* (New York and London: Appleton–Century–Crofts, 1940), pp. 103–107, 128–198.

17. See R. W. Pence, *A Grammar of Present-Day English* (New York: Macmillan, 1950), p. 219, and J. M. Kierzek, *The Macmillan Handbook of English* (3rd ed.; New York: Macmillan, 1954), p. 323. Both writers state that verb forms are identical for subjunctive–indicative with the exception of third person singular present tense forms and forms of the anomolous verb *be;* Kierzek even gives a paradigm of the almost-identical subjunctive.

18. Etsko Kruisinga, *An English Grammar* (Groningen: P. Noordhoff, 1941), I, 587, and general verbal discussions.

19. Bernard Bloch, "English Verb Inflection", *Language,* XXIII (December, 1947), 399–418.

20. The first is quoted by Zandvoort (see Note 6, Introduction); the second is an example sentence from A. H. Marckwardt and F. G. Walcott, *Facts About Current English Usage* (New York and London: Appleton–Century–Crofts, 1938), in a survey of American standards of usage. The sentence was considered by at least 75 per cent of some two

hundred judges as acceptable for literary or good colloquial usage.

21. W. F. Twaddell, *The English Verb Auxiliaries* (Rev. ed.; Providence, R. I.: Brown University Press, 1963), pp. 15, 18, 23.

22. Zandvoort, *A Handbook of English Grammar;* Sledd, *op. cit.*

23. Sledd, *op. cit.*, p. 226.

24. Zandvoort, *op. cit.*, Chapters 4, 5, and 6. The passages quoted are on pages 103, 382, and 106 respectively.

25. Frank Behre, "Notes on Indicative Clauses of Condition", *Contributions to English Syntax and Philology* (Gothenburg: Almqvist & Wiksell, 1962), p. 58.

26. Martin Joos, *The English Verb: Form and Meanings* (Madison: University of Wisconsin Press, 1964), Chapter VI, and pp. 149–150.

27. *Ibid.*, p. 159.

28. Frank Behre, "The Subjunctive in Old English Poetry", *Göteborgs Högskolas Arsskrift,* XI (Göteborg: Wettergren & Kerbers Förlag, 1934), pp. 6–7.

29. Wilde, *op. cit.*, Teil III, 103.

CHAPTER TWO

1. For grammars used for the respective chronological periods, see Appendix A, note 1.

2. Randolph Quirk and C. L. Wrenn, *An Old English Grammar* (London: Methuen & Co. Ltd., 1955), p. 82.

3. Hugh Pope, *English Versions of the Bible,* rev. by Sebastian Bullough (St. Louis and London: Herder, 1952), pp. 46–51; Walter W. Skeat (ed.), *The Gospels in Anglo–Saxon, Northumbrian, and Old Mercian Versions* (Cambridge: University Press, 1871–77), Preface to St. John's Gospel, p. xii.

4. Eduard Sievers, *An Old English Grammar,* trans. A.S. Cook (3rd ed.; Boston: Ginn & Co., 1903), pp. 256–267.

5. W. W. Skeat, "On the Dialect of Wycliffe's Bible", *Transactions of the Philological Society* (London: Kegan Paul, Trench, Trübner & Co., 1898), pp. 212–219.

6. David W. Reed, *The History of Inflectional N in English Verbs Before 1500* ("University of California Publications in English", Vol. 7), Berkeley and Los Angeles: University of California Press, 1950. See Appendix A for a description of this study; Franz J. Ortmann, *Formen und Syntax des Verbs bei Wycliffe und Purvey* (Dissertation, Berlin, 1902), p. 8.

7. Skeat, *The Gospels in Anglo–Saxon, Northumbrian, and Old Mercian Versions,* Preface to St. John's Gospel, p. xiii.

8. Pope, *op. cit.,* pp. 313–327.

9. J. M. Grainger, "Studies in the Syntax of the King James Version", *Studies in Philology,* XI (1907), 1–60.

10. E. J. Goodspeed, *The New Testament, An American Translation* (Chicago: University of Chicago Press, 1923), p. v.

11. See Introduction, note 7.

12. Quirk and Wrenn, *op. cit.,* pp. 83–84.

13. *Ibid.,* p. 54.

CHAPTER THREE

1. Two secondary sources that were used to good effect in classifying verb forms in the *Chronicle* were A. H. Marckwardt, "Verb Inflections in Late Old English", *Philologica: The Malone Anniversary Studies* (Baltimore: Johns Hopkins Press, 1950), pp. 79–88; H. M. Blain, *Syntax of the Verb in the Anglo–Saxon Chronicle from 787 A.D. to 1001 A.D.* (New York: A. S. Barnes & Co., 1901), pp. 24–25. Marckwardt's article contains valuable information concerning the existence in Old English of present and preterite subjunctive plural forms in *–on* and *–an* along with the formerly regular *–en,* with the preterite subjunctive showing predominantly *–on* endings; it notes, further, the substitution of *–an, –en,* or even *–e* for the regular *–on* ending of indicative plural verbs. Consequently, in analyzing plural verbs in the texts it was

frequently necessary to use a system of syntactic comparison with verbs in unambiguous modal structures. Preterite subjunctive plural forms, since they showed no formal contrast with preterite indicative forms, were considered as non-distinctive subjunctive forms. Present tense subjunctive plural forms ending in *–an* or *–on,* since they did show formal contrast with present *aþ* and *eþ* forms, were classified as subjunctives. Indicative preterite plurals ending in *–en* were recorded and, though not incorporated in tabulation of subjunctive statistics, are listed in the textual evidence (Appendix B). Because, as Marckwardt states, ". . . preteritive-present verbs [were often] employed as periphrastic indicators of modal ideas; [they] did not often take the subjunctive form", designation of modal auxiliary constructions in the *Chronicle* required substitution of inflected subjunctive forms. Blain's study calls attention to the use of preterite verb forms with "the meaning of a conditional", listing as examples such structures as: *þa gerædde se cyng and ealle his witan þæt man gegaderode þa scipu* . . . 992E. For purposes of analysis, such structures were designated as modal preterite inflections.

2. In the classification of Middle English verb forms, the following works were of special help: David W. Reed, *The History of Inflectional N in English Verbs Before 1500* (Berkeley and Los Angeles: University of California Press, 1950), p. 159; and the "Introduction" to F. N. Robinson's edition of *The Works of Geoffrey Chaucer* (2nd ed.; Boston: Houghton Mifflin, 1957), pp. xxx–xxxv.

3. Curme, *op. cit.,* p. 390; Zandvoort, *A Handbook of English Grammar,* pp. 102, 382.

4. Blain, *op. cit.*

Chapter Four

1. Asta Kihlboom, "The Present Subjunctive in Conditional Clauses", Studia Neophilologica, XI (1938–39), 262.

2. David W. Reed, *op. cit.*

CHAPTER FIVE

1. Jespersen; see Chapter One, note 12, above.

2. Numbering of quotations from the plays, as explained in Appendix B, is based on lineal designation or, more often, on textual pagination. Lineal designation is indicated.

3. Jespersen, *A Modern English Grammar,* Part VII, p. 626.

4. *Ibid.,* Part VI, p. 133.

5. C. C. Fries, *The Structure of English* (New York: Harcourt, Brace, 1952), p. 103, discusses *let us* and *lets* [sic] as being in separate categories, the form *lets* serving as an introductory expression. Fries does not classify either of these structures as modal auxiliary constructions as I have in this research. On the other hand, in this investigation I considered *let us* an imperative construction.

APPENDIX A

1. Grammars used for the respective chronological periods (Old, Middle, and Modern English) were as follows: Randolph Quirk and C. L. Wrenn, *An Old English Grammar* (London: Methuen, 1955); Joseph Wright and E. M. Wright, *An Elementary Middle English Grammar* (2nd ed.; Oxford: Oxford University Press, 1928); and Henry Sweet, *A New English Grammar, Logical and Historical* (Oxford: Clarendon Press, 1892–98), Vol. 1. See also Hans Kurath and S. H. Kuhn, *Middle English Dictionary* (Ann Arbor: University of Michigan Press, 1952), pp. 8–14.

2. Leonard Bloomfield ("Old English Plural Subjunctives in –e", *Journal of English and Germanic Philology,* XXIX [1930], 100–113) points out the frequent use in Old English manuscripts of the –*n*-less plural subjunctive form, a feature later partially corrected by the scribes. F. A. Wood ("Some Verb Forms in Germanic", *Modern Philology,* XIV [1916],

121–128) traces the development of –*e*-plural subjunctives in antepronominal positions.

3. Marckwardt, "Verb Inflections in Late Old English". See Note 1, Chapter Three.

4. Reed, *op. cit.*

5. *Ibid.,* pp. 194–195, 255–256, 235.

6. Wright and Wright, *op. cit.,* p. 171.

7. Sweet, *op. cit.,* p. 389.

8. Jespersen *(A Modern English Grammar,* Part VI, p. 11) argues that the form –*st* (second person singular present tense) following *thou* should be considered subjunctive. Sweet *(op. cit.,* p. 389) lists identical forms in indicative and subjunctive paradigms for Modern English.

9. Jespersen, *A Modern English Grammar,* Part V, p. 473; Kennedy, *op. cit.,* p. 522.

10. For references to plays quoted see the introduction to Appendix B for the system of citation, which varied somewhat according to text used. Further bibliographical information on dramatic texts is given in the introduction to Chapter V and under Bibliography.

11. Jespersen, *A Modern English Grammar,* Part V, p. 63.

12. *Ibid.,* Part VII, p. 637.

13. See note 10, above.

14. See note 10, above.

15. E. B. Setzler, "Why Not a Future Subjunctive?", *Modern Language Notes,* XXIII (1908), 243–244.

16. Fries, *American English Grammar,* pp. 103–105.

17. Fries, "The Periphrastic Future with SHALL and WILL in Modern English", *Publications of the Modern Language Association,* XL (December, 1925), 963–1024, comments as follows:

> Very probably a speaker or writer seldom conceives of the future event entirely freed from the circumstances upon which it is predicated; and, likewise, for the hearer or reader . . . there often stand out some of the connotations of *intention, resolve, determination, compulsion* or *necessity.* There are,

> without question, unmistakable modal uses of *shall* and *will,*
> but they are mingled with these lighter shades of connotation
> and so inseparably joined to them that no *rules* seem adequate
> to distinguish them satisfactorily.

His comments on the functions and the classification of
auxiliaries are equally perceptive in the article "The Expression of the Future", *Language,* III, No. 2 (1927), 87–95. See
also the discussion in Joos' chapter "Assertion", Chapter
Six, pp. 147–201 (Joos, *op. cit.*).

18. F. Behre, *Meditative–Polemic SHOULD in Modern
English THAT–Clauses* ("Gothenburg Studies in English",
IV [Stockholm: Almqvist & Wiksell, 1955]), p. 101–102.

19. See note 3, Introduction.

20. *The Hairy Ape,* p. 820.

21. *Ibid.,* p. 822.

22. *Gorboduc,* line 69.

23. *The Hairy Ape,* p. 820.

24. C. H. Haile, *Shall and Will and the English Subjunctive* (Richmond: Nicholson Press, 1913), pp. 8, 9.

25. Jespersen, *A Modern English Grammar,* Part V, p. 637.

26. *The Hairy Ape,* p. 824.

27. *Melibee,* line 1038.

28. *All For Love,* p. 19.

29. Kennedy, *op. cit.,* p. 521.

30. G. O. Curme, "The Forms and Functions of the Subjunctive in the Classical and Modern Languages", *Modern
Philology,* XXVI (May, 1929), 387–399.

31. In *A Modern English Grammar,* Part IV, pp. 113ff.,
Jespersen, discussing the preterite used in "Imaginative Use
of Tenses", says in part:

> Originally this use [preterite to denote rejected condition
> and condition contrary to fact] was found in the preterit
> *subjunctive* only, and the unreality was denoted by the
> mood rather than by the tense. But in course of time the
> distinction between the forms of the subjunctive and those

of the indicative came to be blotted out, and now in 99 pct. of cases it is impossible from the form to tell which of the two moods is used, thus with all strong verbs: *came, drank, held,* etc., and with all weak verbs: *ended, sent,* etc. The only form in which the distinction survives, is *was* (ind.) and *were* (subj.), and even here it should be noted that the plural form *were* belongs to both moods. . . . It was, therefore, unavoidable that this last relic of the preterit subjunctive should also give way before the overwhelming pressure of other forms,—the more so, as no inconvenience was ever felt by the fact that there is no corresponding difference in the other verbs—and we see a growing tendency to use *was* in the singular instead of *were* where unreality is to be indicated, though the literary language is here, as usual, more conservative than the spoken language. . . .

32. Behre, "The Subjunctive in Old English Poetry", p. 53.

33. Jespersen, *A Modern English Grammar,* Part V, p. 377.

34. Charleston, *op. cit.,* p. 79.

35. *A Taste of Honey,* p. 13.

36. *All for Love,* p. 19.

37. *Havelok,* lines 152–155.

38. *Ibid.,* line 209.

39. G. Forsström, *The Verb "To Be" in Middle English: A Survey of the Forms* ("Lund Studies in English", Vol. XV [Lund: C. W. K. Gleerup, 1948]), p. 20.

40. *Havelok,* line 338.

41. *Ibid.,* line 824.

42. *Hazel Kirke,* p. 442.

43. Charleston, *op. cit.,* p. 164; Jespersen, *A Modern English Grammar,* Part VII, p. 626.

44. Fries, *The Structure of English,* pp. 74–294.

45. The category added (Number 13) is the relative clause, also called (by Behre [*The Subjunctive in Old English Poetry,* pp. 70, 181ff.]) "adjective clause."

46. Behre, *ibid.,* pp. 9ff., 65ff.

Bibliography

CHRONOLOGICAL LIST OF PRIMARY SOURCES

N. B.—The forty-four texts are listed chronologically according to MS or publication date. MS dates for the first seventeen texts (i.e., up to and including *The Towneley Play of Noah,* 1475) are approximate; thus, the MS date "1475", given for *The Towneley Play . . . ,* should be understood to be *"ca.* 1475". *Dates enclosed in brackets are those of composition or, for some of the dramatic works, of first performance.*

800   [*ca.* 800] British Museum MS, Rushworth (Latin text), and

950   [*ca.* 950] British Museum MS, Rushworth (English gloss), both in "The English Gloss of the Rushworth Gospels", *The Gospels in Anglo–Saxon, Northumbrian, and Old Mercian Versions,* ed. W. W. Skeat. 4 vols. Cambridge: University Press, 1871–77.

1121 or 1122 [*ca.* 1121 or 1122] Oxford MS, Bodley Laud 636 (first hand). *Peterborough Chronicle,* in *Two of the Saxon Chronicles Parallel,* ed. Charles Plummer. 2 vols. Oxford: Clarendon Press, 1892–99.

1160   [*ca.* 1160] Oxford MS, Bodley Laud 636 (last hand). *Peterborough Chronicle,* in *Two of the Saxon Chronicles Parallel,* ed. Charles Plummer. 2 vols. Oxford: Clarendon Press, 1892–99.

1225   [*ca.* 1200?] Oxford MS, Bodley 34. *Hali Meidenhad,* ed. F. J. Furnivall. (Early English Text Society, 18.) Lon-

don: H. Milford for the Oxford University Press, 1922.
1250 [*ca.* 1175?] Oxford MS, Bodley Digby A 4. *Poema Morale*, ed. Julius Zupitza. *Anglia*, I (1878), 6–32.
1250? [*ca.* 1175?] British Museum MS, Egerton 613, Fol. 7. *Poema Morale*, in *Old English Homilies* (First Series), ed. Richard Morris. (Early English Text Society, 29, 34.) London: N. Trübner & Company, 1868.
1325 [*ca.* 1300] Oxford MS, Bodley Laud Miscellany 108. *The Lay of Havelok the Dane* (2nd ed.), ed. W. W. Skeat, rev. Kenneth Sisam. Oxford: Clarendon Press, 1915.
1340 [*ca.* 1325] British Museum MS, Cotton Vespasian A 3. *Cursor Mundi*, ed. Richard Morris. 7 vols. (Early English Text Society 57, 59, 62, 66, 68, 99, 101.) London: Kegan Paul, Trench, Trübner & Co., 1874–93.
1350 [1340] British Museum MS, Arundel 57. Michel, Dan. *Ayenbit of Inwyt*, ed. Richard Morris. (Early English Text Society, 23.) London: N. Trübner & Co., 1866.
1389 [*ca.* 1380] *The Gospel of Matheu, Mark, Luke, and Joon in Englische* (Wycliffe translations), in *The Gospels, Gothic, Anglo–Saxon, Wycliffe, and Tyndale Versions* (4th ed.), ed. Joseph Bosworth and George Waring. London: J. R. Smith, 1907.
1387–92 [*ca.* 1387–92] Chaucer, Geoffrey. *The Tale of Melibee, The Parson's Tale* from *The Canterbury Tales*, in *The Works of Geoffrey Chaucer* (2nd ed.), ed. F. N. Robinson. Boston: Houghton Mifflin Company, 1957.
1400 [*ca.* 1343–*ca.* 1349] Cambridge MS, Dd. V 64. "The Form of Living", in *Richard Rolle of Hampole and His Followers*, ed. Carl Horstmann. 2 vols. ("Yorkshire Writers Series".) London: Sonnenschein & Co., 1896.
1400 [*ca.* 1387] Cambridge MS, St. John's College H 1. *John of Trevisa's Translation of Ralph Higden's Polychronicon*, ed. E. S. Babington. 9 vols. ("Rolls Series", 41.) London: Longman & Co., 1865–86.
1400 [*ca.* 1390–1400?] British Museum MS, Cotton Nero A 10. *Sir Gawain and the Green Knight*, ed. J. R. R. Tolkien and E. V. Gordon. Oxford: Clarendon Press, 1925.
1430–40 [1340–50] British Museum MS, Additional 35290. York Cycle. *Harrowing of Hell*, ed. L. T. Smith (1885), in *Fourteenth Century Verse and Prose*, ed. Kenneth Sisam. Oxford: Clarendon Press, 1921.
1475 [1400] Towneley MS, Towneley Miracles. *The Towne-*

ley Play of Noah, ed. George England and Alfred W. Pollard (1897), in *Fourteenth Century Verse and Prose,* ed. Kenneth Sisam. Oxford: Clarendon Press, 1921.

1526 *The Gospell of S. Mathew, S. Marke, S. Luke, and S. Ihon* (Tyndale translation), in *The Gospels, Gothic, Anglo–Saxon, Wycliffe, and Tyndale Versions* (4th ed.), ed. Joseph Bosworth and George Waring. London: J. R. Smith, 1907.

1566 [1553–54] Udall, Nicholas. *Ralph Roister Doister,* in *Minor Elizabethan Drama* (Vol. 2), ed. A. H. Thorndyke. ("Everyman's Library", No. 492.) London: J. M. Dent & Sons, and New York: E. P. Dutton & Co., 1910.

1562 [1560] Norton, Thomas, and Sackville, Thomas. *Gorboduc,* in *Minor Elizabethan Drama* (Vol. 1), ed. A. H. Thorndyke. ("Everyman's Library", No. 491.) London: J. M. Dent & Sons and New York: E. P. Dutton & Co., 1910.

1604 [1589] Marlowe, Christopher. *The Tragical History of Doctor Faustus* in *Marlowe's Dr. Faustus and Goethe's Faust* (Part 1), ed. A. W. Ward. Oxford: H. Milford for the Oxford University Press, 1907.

1611 *The Holy Bible, Authorized King James Version.* New York: Thomas Nelson & Sons, 1936.

1623 [1591] Shakespeare, William. *Two Gentlemen of Verona,* in *William Shakespeare, The Complete Works,* ed. Peter Alexander. London: Collins, 1951.

1676 Etherege, Sir George. *The Man of Mode,* in *Restoration Plays,* ed. Edmund Gosse. London: J. M. Dent & Sons and New York: E. P. Dutton & Co., 1932.

1678 Dryden, John. *All for Love,* in *Restoration Plays,* ed. Edmund Gosse. London: J. M. Dent & Sons and New York: E. P. Dutton & Co., 1932.

1723 [1722] Steele, Sir Richard. *The Conscious Lovers,* in *English Plays 1660–1820,* ed. A. E. Morgan. New York and London: Harper & Brothers, 1935.

1731 Lillo, George. *The London Merchant: or, The History of George Barnwell,* in *English Plays 1660–1820,* ed. A. E. Morgan. New York and London: Harper & Brothers, 1935.

1773 Goldsmith, Oliver. *She Stoops to Conquer or The Mistakes of a Night,* in *The Vicar of Wakefield and Other Writings,* ed. F. W. Hilles. New York: Dutton, 1955.

1777 Sheridan, R. B. *The School for Scandal,* in *English Lit-*

erature and its Backgrounds, ed. B. D. Grebanier, *et al.* New York: Dryden Press, 1949.

1815 Peacock, T. L. *The Three Doctors,* in *The Plays of Thomas Love Peacock,* ed. by A. B. Young. London: D. Nutt, 1910.

1824 Irving, W. and Payne, J. H. *Charles the Second; or the Merry Monarch,* in *Representative American Plays from 1767 to the Present Day* (5th ed.), ed. A. H. Quinn. New York: Appleton–Century Co., 1930.

1877 Tennyson, Alfred Lord. *Harold, A Drama.* Boston: J. R. Osgood & Co., 1877.

1880 MacKaye, J. S. *Hazel Kirke,* in *Representative American Plays from 1767 to the Present Day* (5th ed.), ed. A. H. Quinn. New York: Appleton–Century Co., 1930.

1893 Pinero, Sir Arthur. *The Second Mrs. Tanqueray,* in *The Development of English Drama,* ed. G. E. Bentley. New York: Appleton–Century–Crofts, 1950.

1897 [1888] Howard, Bronson. *Shenandoah,* in *Representative American Plays from 1767 to the Present Day* (7th ed.), ed. A. H. Quinn. New York: Appleton–Century–Crofts, 1953.

1922 O'Neill, Eugene. *The Hairy Ape,* in *A Treasury of the Theater,* ed. John Gassner. New York: Simon & Schuster, 1956.

1923 *The New Testament, An American Translation.* Translated by E. J. Goodspeed. Chicago: University of Chicago Press, 1923.

1929 Maugham, W. S. *The Sacred Flame,* in *The Collected Plays of William Somerset Maugham* (Vol. 3). London: W. Heinemann Ltd., 1931.

1934 [1931] *The Tale of Melibeus* and *The Parson's Tale,* both in *The Canterbury Tales.* Translated by J. U. Nicolson. Garden City: Garden City Publishing Co., 1936.

1947 [1946] Haines, W. W. *Command Decision,* in *Representative American Plays from 1767 to the Present Day* (7th ed.), ed. A. H. Quinn. New York: Appleton–Century–Crofts, 1953.

1949 Miller, Arthur. *Death of a Salesman,* in *A Treasury of the Theater,* ed. John Gassner. New York: Simon & Schuster, 1956.

1953 *The Anglo–Saxon Chronicle.* Translated by G. N. Garmonsway. Revised edition. London: J. M. Dent & Sons and New York: E. P. Dutton & Co., 1953.

1959   Delaney, Shelagh. *A Taste of Honey*. London: Grove
        Press, 1959.
1961   Osborne, John. *A Subject of Scandal and Concern*.
        London: Faber & Faber, 1961.

SECONDARY SOURCES

Adams, Arthur. *The Syntax of the Temporal Clause in Old
    English Prose*. ("Yale Studies in English", XXXII.) New
    York: Henry Holt & Co., 1907.
Baugh, A. C. *A History of the English Language* (2nd ed.).
    New York: Appleton–Century–Crofts, 1957.
Behre, Frank. *Meditative-Polemic SHOULD in Modern Eng-
    lish THAT–Clauses*. ("Gothenburg Studies in English",
    IV.) Stockholm: Almqvist & Wiksell, 1955.
_____. "Notes on Indicative Clauses of Condition", *Contri-
    butions to English Syntax and Philology*. Gothenburg: Alm-
    qvist & Wiksell, 1962.
_____. "The Subjunctive in Old English Poetry" (*Göte-
    borgs Högskolas Arsskrift, XI*), Göteborg: Wettergren &
    Kerbers Förlag, 1934.
Blain, H. M. *Syntax of the Verb in the Anglo–Saxon Chron-
    icle from 787 A. D. to 1001 A. D.* New York: A. S. Barnes
    & Co., 1901.
Bloch, Bernard. "English Verb Inflection", *Language*, XXIII
    (December, 1947), 399–418.
Bloomfield, Leonard. *Language*. New York: Henry Holt & Co.,
    1933.
_____. "Old English Plural Subjunctives in –e", *Journal of
    English and Germanic Philology* (Urbana), XXIX (Jan-
    uary, 1930), 100–113.
Bosworth, Joseph, and Toller, N. T. *An Anglo–Saxon Dic-
    tionary*. Oxford: Clarendon Press, 1882–98. Supplement,
    Clarendon Press, 1908.
Brown, Goold. *The Grammar of English Grammars*. New
    York: W. Wood, 1862.
Burnham, J. M. *Concessive Constructions in Old English Prose*.
    ("Yale Studies in English", XXXIX.) New York: Henry
    Holt & Co., 1911.
Callaway, Morgan, Jr. *The Consecutive Subjunctive in Old
    English*. Boston: D. C. Heath & Co., 1933.
_____. *The Temporal Subjunctive in Old English*. Austin:
    University of Texas, 1931.

Charleston, Britta Marian. *Studies on the Syntax of the English Verb*. ("Swiss Studies in English.") Bern: A. Francke A.G., 1941.

Curme, G. O. "The Forms and Functions of the Subjunctive in the Classical and Modern Languages", *Modern Philology*, XXVI (May, 1929), 387–399.

_____. "Musings Upon the English and the German Subjunctive", *Journal of English and Germanic Philology*, XXX (January, 1931), 1–5.

_____, and Kurath, Hans. *A Grammar of the English Language*. 3 vols. Boston: D. C. Heath & Co., 1931–35.

Emerson, O. F. *The History of the English Language*. New York: Macmillan & Co., 1922.

Fries, C. C. *American English Grammar*. New York and London: Appleton–Century–Crofts, 1940.

_____. "The Expression of the Future", *Language*, III, No. 2 (June, 1927), 87–95.

_____. "The Periphrastic Future with SHALL and WILL in Modern English", *Publications of the Modern Language Association*, XL (December, 1925), 963–1024.

_____. *The Structure of English*. New York: Harcourt, Brace and World, 1952.

Forsström, Gösta. *The Verb "To Be" in Middle English: A Survey of the Forms*. ("Lund Studies in English", XV.) Lund: C. W. K. Gleerup, 1948.

Fowler, H. W. *A Dictionary of Modern English Usage*. Oxford: Clarendon Press, 1926. Rev. ed. Gowers, Sir Ernest, Oxford: Clarendon Press, 1965.

Grainger, J. M. "Studies in the Syntax of the King James Version", *Studies in Philology*, XI (1907), 1–60.

Haile, C. H. *SHALL and WILL and the English Subjunctive*. Richmond: Nicholson Press, 1913.

Hettich, E. L., and Maitland, A. G. C. *Latin Fundamentals* (3rd ed.). Englewood Cliffs: Prentice–Hall, 1958.

Hirtle, W. H. "The English Present Subjunctive", *Canadian Journal of Linguistics*, IX (1964), 75–82.

House, H. C., and Harman, S. E. *Descriptive English Grammar*. New York: Prentice–Hall, 1950.

Jesperson, Otto. *Essentials of English Grammar*. London: G. Allen & Unwin, 1933.

_____. *A Modern English Grammar on Historical Principles*. (7 vols.) London: G. Allen & Unwin, 1954.

_____. *The Philosophy of Grammar*. London: G. Allen & Unwin, 1924.

Joos, Martin. *The English Verb: Form and Meanings.* Madison: University of Wisconsin Press, 1964.

Kantor, J. R. *An Objective Psychology of Grammar.* Bloomington: Indiana University Press, 1952.

Kellner, Leon, *Historical Outlines of English Syntax.* London: Macmillan & Co., 1892.

Kennedy, A. G. *Current English.* Boston: Ginn & Co., 1935.

Kierzek, J. M. *The Macmillan Handbook of English* (3rd ed.). New York: The Macmillan Company, 1954.

Kihlboom, A. M. "The Present Subjunctive in Conditional Clauses", *Studia Neophilologica,* XI (1938–39), 263–268.

Kruisinga, Etsko, and Erades, P. A., *An English Grammar* (Vol. 1) Groningen: P. Noordhoff, 1941.

_____. *A Handbook of Present-Day English* (5th ed.). 3 vols. Groningen: P. Noordhoff, 1932.

Kurath, Hans, and Kuhn, S. H. *Middle English Dictionary.* Ann Arbor: University of Michigan Press, 1952.

Marckwardt, A. H. "Verb Inflection in Late Old English", *Philologica: The Malone Anniversary Studies.* Baltimore: Johns Hopkins Press, 1950, pp. 79–89.

_____, and Walcott, F. G. *Facts About Current English Usage.* New York and London: Appleton–Century–Crofts, 1938.

Mayhew, A. L., and Skeat, W. W. *A Concise Dictionary of Middle English.* Oxford: Clarendon Press, 1888.

Moore, Samuel. *Historical Outlines of English Phonology and Morphology* (2nd ed.). Ann Arbor: G. Wahr, 1925.

Nesbitt, Catherine M. "The Whim of the Moment", *Die Neueren Sprachen,* No. 5 (1961), 238–244.

Ortmann, F. J. *Formen und Syntax des Verbs bei Wycliffe und Purvey.* Dissertation, Berlin, 1902.

Pence, R. W. *A Grammar of Present-Day English.* New York: Macmillan, 1950.

Pope, the Very Reverend Hugh. *English Versions of the Bible.* Revised by the Reverend Sebastian Bullough, O. P. St. Louis and London: Herder, 1952.

Poutsma, Hendrik. *A Grammar of Late Modern English.* 5 vols. Groningen: P. Noordhoff , 1926.

_____. *Mood and Tense of the English Verb.* Groningen: P. Noordhoff, 1922.

Quirk, Randolph, and Wrenn, C. L., *An Old English Grammar.* London: Methuen & Co. Ltd., 1955.

Reed, David W. *The History of Inflectional N in English Verbs Before 1500.* ("University of California Publications in English", Vol. 7.) Berkeley and Los Angeles: University of California Press, 1950.

Ryan, W. M. "More on Pseudo–Subjunctive 'Were' ", *American Speech*, XXXVII (1962), 114–122.

Setzler, E. B. "Why Not a Future Subjunctive?" *Modern Language Notes*, XXIII (December, 1908), 243–244.

Shearin, H. G. *The Expression of Purpose in Old English Prose.* ("Yale Studies in English", XVIII.) New York: Henry Holt & Co., 1903.

————. "The Expression of Purpose in the Authorized Version of the Bible", *Archiv für das Studium der Neueren Sprachen*, CXXI (1908), 297–316.

Sievers, Eduard. *An Old English Grammar* (3rd ed.). Translated by A. S. Cook. Boston: Ginn & Co., 1903.

Simpson, D. P. *Cassell's New Latin–English English–Latin Dictionary.* London: Cassell, 1953.

Skeat, W. W. "On the Dialect of Wycliffe's Bible", *Transactions of the Philological Society.* London: Kegan Paul, Trench, Trübner & Co., 1898.

Sledd, James H. *A Short Introduction to English Grammar.* Chicago: Scott, Foresman & Co., 1959.

Sweet, Henry. *A New English Grammar, Logical and Historical.* 2 vols. Oxford: Clarendon Press, 1892–98.

————. *Student's Dictionary of Anglo–Saxon.* New York: Macmillan Co., 1897.

Twaddell, W. F. *The English Verb Auxiliaries.* Revised edition. Providence, R.I.: Brown University Press, 1963.

Wilde, Hans–Oskar. "Aufforderung, Wunsch und Möglichkeit", *Anglia*, LXIII (1939), 209–389, and LXIV (1940), 10–105.

Wolff, A. *Zur Syntax des Verbums in Altenglischen Lay of Havelok the Dane.* Foreign Dissertation. Leipzig, 1909.

Wood, Francis A. "Some Verb Forms in Germanic", *Modern Philology*, XIV (June, 1916), 121–128.

Wright, J., and Wright, E. M. *An Elementary Middle English Grammar* (2nd ed.). Oxford: H. Milford for the Oxford University Press, 1928.

Zandvoort, R. W. *A Handbook of English Grammar* (7th ed.). Groningen: J. B. Wolters, 1959.

————. "On the So-Called Subjunctive", *English Language Teaching*, XVII (January, 1963), 73–77.

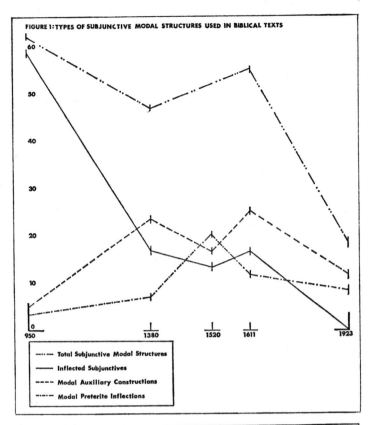

FIGURE 1: TYPES OF SUBJUNCTIVE MODAL STRUCTURES USED IN BIBLICAL TEXTS

-··-··- Total Subjunctive Modal Structures
———— Inflected Subjunctives
- - - - Modal Auxiliary Constructions
-·-·- Modal Preterite Inflections

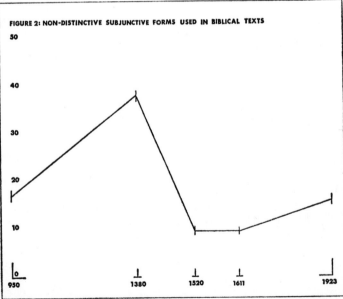

FIGURE 2: NON-DISTINCTIVE SUBJUNCTIVE FORMS USED IN BIBLICAL TEXTS

FIGURE 3: SUBJUNCTIVE MODAL STRUCTURES IN BIBLICAL TEXTS, LISTED BY SYNTACTIC CATEGORY

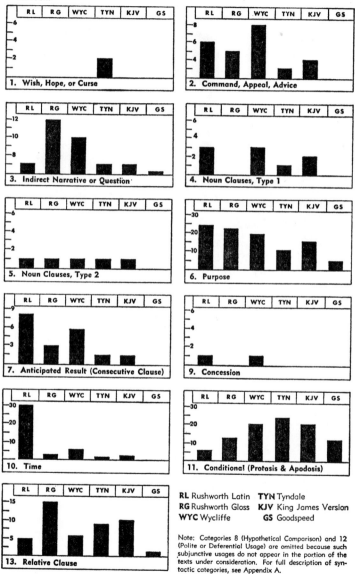

RL Rushworth Latin   TYN Tyndale
RG Rushworth Gloss   KJV King James Version
WYC Wycliffe   GS Goodspeed

Note: Categories 8 (Hypothetical Comparison) and 12 (Polite or Deferential Usage) are omitted because such subjunctive usages do not appear in the portion of the texts under consideration. For full description of syntactic categories, see Appendix A.

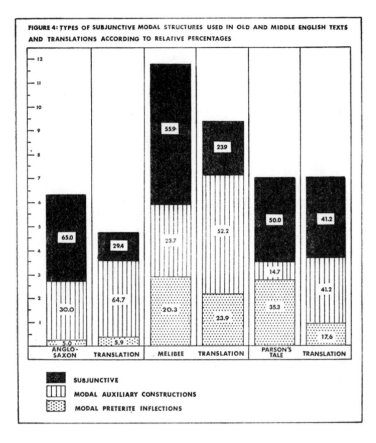

FIGURE 4: TYPES OF SUBJUNCTIVE MODAL STRUCTURES USED IN OLD AND MIDDLE ENGLISH TEXTS AND TRANSLATIONS ACCORDING TO RELATIVE PERCENTAGES

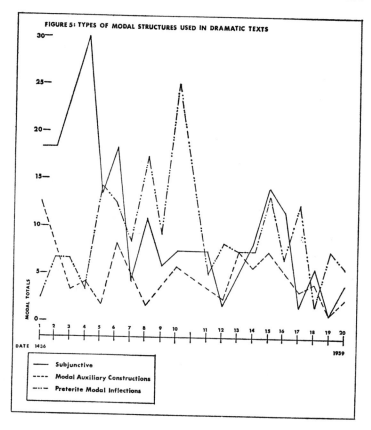

FIGURE 5: TYPES OF MODAL STRUCTURES USED IN DRAMATIC TEXTS

——— Subjunctive
----- Modal Auxiliary Constructions
—··— Preterite Modal Inflections

Table 1: Type and Category of Subjunctive Modal Structures in Biblical Translations

Version: Total Verbs: Modal Type* (Subtotals in italics) Category:	Rushworth Latin (964)				Rushworth Gloss (1,010)				Wycliffe (976)				Tyndale (1,074)				King James (1,058)				Goodspeed (1,079)			
	S	M	P	N	S	M	P	N	S	M	P	N	S	M	P	N	S	M	P	N	S	M	P	N
1. Wish	6				5																			
2. Command	7				6	1			5				2				2			4				
3. Indirect Narrative	3				5				2	3	1	4	1	4	1	1	1	4	1	1		1	1	
4. Noun Clause 1	1				1				1			2	1					1	1					
5. Noun Clause 2	23				17	5			1	3		1	1	4	5	1	1	7						
6. Purpose	8				2	1			3	6		11	1	4	5		1	7	5	13	2	1		3
7. Result									1	1			1	1			1	1		1				
8. Comparison	1											1												
9. Concession	30				12			2	1	3		3	1				2							
10. Time	6				6			1	3	12	3	21	7	3	12	2	2	8	8	20	7	3	2	12
11. Conditional																								
12. Polite Usage													2											
13. Relative Clause	5				5	2	2	6	1	3	2	6	6		2	8	1	6	2	9	1	1		2
Total:	90			*90*	59	4	2	14 *79*	18	24	6	31 *79*	14	17	22	3 *56*	18	26	12	3 *59*	10	6	3	*19*
Non-Subjunctives:	*43*				*54*				*54*				*77*				*74*				*114*			
GRAND TOTAL:	133				133				133				133				133				133			

*Modal Type: S = Subjunctive; M = Modal Auxiliary Construction; P = Modal Preterite Inflection; N = Nondistinctive Subjunctive Structure.

Table 2: Relative Percentages of Modal Forms in Biblical Translations

Percentages of Subjunctive Modal Forms According to Type

Version:	Rushworth Latin	Rushworth Gloss	Wycliffe	Tyndale	King James	Goodspeed
Subjunctive	100	91	37.5	26.5	32.2	0
Modal Auxiliary Construction	0	6	50.0	32.0	46.4	62.5
Modal Preterite Inflection	0	3	12.5	41.5	21.4	37.5

Percentages of Non-Distinctive Modal Forms Per Total Subjunctive Modal Structures

Version:	Rushworth Latin	Rushworth Gloss	Wycliffe	Tyndale	King James	Goodspeed
Subjunctive	0	17.7	39.2	5.3	5.1	15.8

Percentages of Inflected and of Subjunctive Modal Structures Per Total Finite Verb Constructions

Version:	Rushworth Latin	Rushworth Gloss	Wycliffe	Tyndale	King James	Goodspeed
Subjunctive	9.3	5.8	1.8	1.3	1.7	0
Subjunctive Modal Structure	9.3	6.4	4.9	4.9	5.3	5.1

Table 3: Non-Subjunctive Structures Which Alternate with a Subjunctive Structure in Biblical Texts

Form	Version: Subjunctive Category	Rushworth Latin	Rushworth Gloss	Wycliffe	Tyndale	King James	Goodspeed
Indicative Mood	Command	2	2	2	2	4	3
	Indirect Narrative	5	1	3	4	4	3
	Noun Clause 1	3			4	4	2
	Purpose		6	3	4	7	5
	Result		1		7		7
	Concession				1		1
	Time	18	28	26	28	26	29
	Conditional	8	10	3	1	1	12
	Relative Clause			8	5	5	9
	Totals	*36*	*48*	*45*	*56*	*51*	*71*
Imperative Mood	Command		1	1	1	1	2
	Indirect Narrative				1	1	1
	Purpose	1	1	1	1	1	1
	Totals	*1*	*2*	*2*	*3*	*3*	*4*
Infinitive Mood Construction	Indirect Narrative	1		1	1	1	3
	Noun Clause 1				1		4
	Noun Clause 2				1		1
	Purpose			3	9	5	10
	Result	1		1	1	1	2
	Relative Clause				1	1	3
	Totals	*2*		*5*	*14*	*8*	*23*

	1	2	3	4	5	6
Prepositional Phrase						
Indirect Narrative					1	1
Purpose					2	2
Totals					3	3
Participle						
Purpose	1	1		1		
Concession						
Time	2			2		1
Relative Clause	3					
Totals	2		3		3	
"Let" Imperative Construction			3			1
Command						
Indirect Narrative						3
Purpose						1
Conditional			3		3	1
Totals						6
Wish						
Indirect Narrative	2	2	2	2		2
Purpose						1
Relative Clause						2
Totals						6
Changed Construction (Noun, Adverb, Zero-Form)	2	2	2	1	1	6
Grand Totals	43	54	54	77	74	114

Table 4: Type and Category of Subjunctive Modal Structures in Old and Middle English Texts and Translations

Modal Type*: Category:	Anglo-Saxon Chronicle S	M	P	N	Translation S	M	P	N	Melibee S	M	P	N	Translation S	M	P	N	Parson's Tale S	M	P	N	Translation S	M	P	N
1. Wish	11		1	*12*			2	10	2			*2*		1	1	1		1	1	*2*		2		*2*
2. Command	5			*5*		2		3				*4*					1	1		*1*				
3. Indirect Narrative	5	14	2	6 *27*		9	3	*12*	2	3	2	5 *10*		1		1	1	1	1	*3*	1	1	1	*3*
4. Noun Clause 1	22	1		*23*	5	6	1	*12*	2	3		*7*		1		7	1	1	1	*7*				
5. Noun Clause 2	5	5	1			5	3	*6*	2	1		*3*				3	1	1		*3*	1	1		*2*
6. Purpose	6		1			3		*3*												*1*				
7. Result	1		1	*7*	2	4		*6*	3		1	5 *5*	1	2		4		1		*1*	1	1		*1*
8. Comparison	4	1		*5*	1	1		*1*	11	2	1	13 *13*	3	2		5	4	2	2 1	*7*	3		2	*5*
9. Concession	1		1	*5*	3			*3*	3			*3*	1			1	2			*2*	2			*2*
10. Time	1	1	2	*2*					9	8	11 5	33 *33*	5	7	10	22	7	3	6	*16*	7	5	3	*15*
11. Conditional	4	2	3 2	*11*	3	4	3	*10*																
12. Polite Usage																								
13. Relative Clause	6	2	1	*10*	1	3		*4*	1			*1*	1	1		1	1	2		*3*	4	4		*4*
14. Ad Hoc																								
Total:	65	30	5 13	*113*	20	44	4 4	*72*	33	14	12 15	*74*	11	24	11	*46*	18	5	12 2	*37*	14	14	6	*34*
Non-Subjunctives:			4				45				3				31				2				5	
GRAND TOTAL:			117				117				77				77				77				39	

*Modal Type: S = Subjunctive; M = Modal Auxiliary Construction; P = Modal Preterite Inflection; N = Non-Distinctive Subjunctive.

Table 5: Relative Percentages of Modal Forms in Old and Middle English Texts and Translations

Percentages of Subjunctive Modal Forms According to Type

	Anglo-Saxon Chronicle	Translation	Melibee	Translation	Parson's Tale	Translation
Subjunctive:	65.0	29.4	55.9	23.9	51.4	41.2
Modal Auxiliary Construction:	30.0	64.7	23.7	52.2	14.3	41.2
Modal Preterite Inflection:	5.0	5.9	20.3	23.9	34.3	17.6

Percentages of Non-Distinctive Modal Forms Per Total Subjunctive Modal Structures

	Anglo-Saxon Chronicle	Translation	Melibee	Translation	Parson's Tale	Translation
	11.5	5.5	20.3	0	5.4	0

Percentages of Inflected Subjunctives and of Subjunctive Modal Structures Per Total Finite Verb Structures

	Anglo-Saxon Chronicle	Translation	Melibee	Translation	Parson's Tale	Translation
Subjunctives:	4.33	1.33	6.6	2.2	3.6	2.8
Subjunctive Modal Structures:	6.6	4.5	11.8	9.2	7.0	6.8

Table 6: Non-Subjunctive Structures that Alternate with a Subjunctive Structure in Old and Middle English Texts and Translations

Form / Subjunctive Category	Anglo-Saxon Chronicle	Translation	Melibee	Translation	Parson's Tale	Translation
Indicative Mood						
Indirect Narrative		4		4		
Noun Clause 1	1	4				
Noun Clause 2						1
Result		1				
Comparison		1		1		
Concession		2		4		1
Time		2		1	1	
Conditional	1					
Relative Clause	2	7		8		
Total	*4*	*21*		*18*	*1*	*2*
Imperative Mood						
Noun Clause			2	1		
Conditional				1		
Total			*2*	*2*		
Infinitive Construction						
Indirect Narrative		10				1
Noun Clause 1		7				
Purpose		2				
Total		*19*				*1*
Prepositional Phrase						
Indirect Narrative				1		
Concession			1		1	
Total			*1*	*1*	*1*	

Participle				
Indirect Narrative		1	1	1
Total		1	1	
"Let" Imperative Construction				
Command		2		
Conditional				
Total		2		
Noun, Adverb, or Conjunction				
Indirect Narrative		1		
Concession			2	
Time			5	
Conditional			1	1
Relative Clause			1	
Total	4	1 2	9 31	2
Grand Total		45		1 2 5

Table 7: Type and Category of Subjunctive Modal Structures in Middle English Texts

Modal Type* (Subtotals in ital.)	Northern			East Midland			West Midland	
	1 Cursor Mundi S M P N	*2* Form of Living S M P N		*3* Ptrbrgh. Chron. S M P N	*4* Havelok S M P N		*5* Hali Meidenhad S M P N	*6* Gawain S M P N
Category:								
1. Wish	2 *9 11*	*1*	7 *1*	7 *1*	14 *2 16*		2 *2 4*	1 *1 2*
2. Command				13 *1 14*	1 6 *2 9*		1 1 *1 2*	2 *2*
3. Indirect Narrative	2 2	1 3 *1 3*			1 2 *3*		4 4 *4*	1 2 *3*
4. Noun Clause 1	1 2 *4 7*	4 1 *5*	5					
5. Noun Clause 2	2 *1 1*	2 *2 15*	2 1 1 *2*		2 5 *1 8*		2 2 *2*	2 *2*
6. Purpose	1 3 *3*	8 3 *4 2*	1 1 *4 3*	2 3 *3*	1 *2 3*		6 1 7 *1*	*1*
7. Result		1 *3 2*	4 1 *1*	2 3 *2*	4 1 *5*		*5*	2 *2*
8. Comparison	1 *2 5*	1 *1 1*	2 *2*	2 4 *6*	6 1 1 *8*		2 *2 4*	
9. Concession	2 1 *1 2*	2 1 *2 1*	1 1 *1*	2 2 *2*	5 7 *2 14*		2 1 2 *2*	2 1 *2 3*
10. Time	1 *2 5*	1 *1 45*	1 2 *1*	2 2 *2 5*	5 2 4 *5 16*		16 3 3 *22*	5 5 1 *1 12*
11. Conditional	3	13 9 5 *18 45*					40 4 5 6 *55*	
12. Polite Usage					1			
13. Relative Clause		1 *1*	1 *1*	1 *1*	3 *3*		1 1 1 1 *4*	1 *1*
14. Ad Hoc					*1*			2 *2*
Total:	5 10 1 22 *38*	30 15 6 27 *78*	17 21 1 8 *47*	40 23 4 17 *84*	40 4 5 6 *55*			11 9 5 13 *38*

*Modal Type: S = Subjunctive; M = Modal Auxiliary Construction; P = Modal Preterite Inflection; N = Non-Distinctive Subjunctive.

Table 7: (continued)

Modal Type*: (Subtotals in italics)	Southeastern									Southwestern									
	7 Poema Morale (Dig.)					8 Ayenbit of Inwyt					9 Poema Morale (Eg.)					10 John of Trevisa's Trans.				
Category:	S	M	P	N		S	M	P	N		S	M	P	N		S	M	P	N	
1. Wish	7				*7*						8				*8*	1				*1*
2. Command	12			6	*18*						10			10	*20*					
3. Indirect Narrative	1	1			*2*			2		*2*	1	1			*2*					
4. Noun Clause 1	2	1			*3*		1			*1*	2	2			*4*		1			*1*
5. Noun Clause 2						1	2			*3*									1	*1*
6. Purpose		2			*2*	2	1			*3*		2			*2*	5				*5*
7. Result						1				*1*			1		*1*			2		*2*
8. Comparison	2				*2*	6				*6*	2				*2*	5	3			*8*
9. Concession	5		1		*6*						4			1	*5*		1		2	*3*
10. Time				2	*2*	1				*1*	1			4	*5*					
11. Conditional	2	6	20	4	*32*				2	*2*	2	7	23	2	*34*			3	2	*5*
12. Polite Usage																				
13. Relative Clause	1			6	*7*						2	2		3	*7*	2	1	1		*4*
14. Ad Hoc	1				*1*	2				*2*	1				*1*					
Total:	33	10	21	18	*82*	13	4	2	2	*21*	33	14	24	20	*91*	13	6	6	5	*30*

*Modal Type: S = Subjunctive; M = Modal Auxiliary Construction; P = Modal Preterite Inflection; N = Non-Distinctive Subjunctive.

Table 8: Relative Percentages of Modal Forms in Middle English Texts

Percentages of Subjunctive Modal Forms According to Type

	1 Cursor Mundi	2 Form of Living	3 Prbrgh. Chronicle	4 Havelock	5 Hali Meidenhad	6 Gawain	7 Poema Morale	8 Ayenbit of Inwyt	9 Poema Morale	10 John of Trevisa's Translation
Subjunctive Modal Auxiliary Construction	31.2	58.8	43.6	59.7	81.6	44.0	51.6	68.4	46.5	52.0
Modal Preterite Inflection	62.5	29.4	53.8	34.3	8.2	36.0	15.6	21.1	19.7	24.0
Non-Distinctive	6.3	11.8	2.6	6.0	10.2	20.0	32.8	10.5	33.8	24.0

Percentages of Non-Distinctive Modal Forms Per Total Subjunctive Modal Structures

	Cursor Mundi	Form of Living	Prbrgh. Chronicle	Havelock	Hali Meidenhad	Gawain	Poema Morale	Ayenbit of Inwyt	Poema Morale	John of Trevisa's Translation
	57.8	34.6	17.0	20.2	10.9	34.2	22.0	9.5	22.0	16.6

Percentages of Inflected Subjunctives and of Total Subjunctive Modal Structures Per Total Finite Verb Structures

	Cursor Mundi	Form of Living	Prbrgh. Chronicle	Havelock	Hali Meidenhad	Gawain	Poema Morale	Ayenbit of Inwyt	Poema Morale	John of Trevisa's Translation
Subjunctive	1.0	6.0	3.4	8.0	8.0	2.2	6.6	2.6	6.6	2.6
Subjunctive Modal Structure	3.2	10.2	7.8	13.4	8.2	5.0	12.8	3.8	14.2	5.0

Table 9: Type and Category of Subjunctive Modal Structures in Dramatic Texts

Number of Text:	1				2				3				4				5			
Modal Type*:	S	M	P	N	S	M	P	N	S	M	P	N	S	M	P	N	S	M	P	N
Category:																				
1. Wish-Curse	2	1		2 5	10			19	5				5	2	1 1	4	6	1	1	7
2. Command				4	4	4									3					
3. Indirect Narrative	4							1	1					3						
4. Noun Clause 1	4	2		1 7	3		3	6	1	2	1	4	4		7	2	2			
5. Noun Clause 2	2			2					1		1		3		1	1				
6. Purpose	1	2		1 4	1		1	2					4	3			2			2
7. Result												1	1		1					
8. Comparison	1			1	1			1		1		1		3		1	1	1		2
9. Concession			2	4	1			2	3			3	3		3	4	2		4	
10. Time	2				1			1	1			1	6		6	2			2	
11. Conditional	7	2	2	1 12	6	3	3	5 17	10		4	14	10	1	2	1 14	5	1	13	19
12. Polite Usage																				
13. Relative Clause																	1			1
14. Ad Hoc	1			2	1		1	2	2	1		3	1		1		2		1	3
Total:	18	13	2	8 41	18	8	7	20 53	23	3		7 33	30	4	3	2 39	23	1	14	2 40

*Modal Type: S = Subjunctive; M = Modal Auxiliary Construction; P = Modal Preterite Inflection; N = Non-Distinctive Subjunctive.

Table 9: (continued)

Number of Text:	6				7				8				9				10			
Modal Type*:	S	M	P	N	S	M	P	N	S	M	P	N	S	M	P	N	S	M	P	N
Category:																				
1. Wish-Curse	1	2	3	1 *7*	1			4 *5*	3		1	*4*		1		*1*	1			*1*
2. Command									2			*2*								
3. Indirect Narrative	1			*1*						1		*1*								
4. Noun Clause 1		3		*5*			1	*1*	1		2	*3*	1	1	2	*4*	1	1	4	*6*
5. Noun Clause 2		1		*1*							1	*1*	1	1	1	*2*			2	*2*
6. Purpose	3	1		*4*	2				1		1	*1*		1		*1*	1	1	1	*1*
7. Result								1 *1*							1 *1*					
8. Comparison									1		1	*2*			4	*4*	1	1	1	*1*
9. Concession														1		*1*	1	1	1	*1*
10. Time	2			*2*							1	*1*								
11. Conditional	10	2	4	5 *21*	3	1	7	1 *12*	4		9	*13*	1	1	2	*4*	4	3	18	1 *26*
12. Polite Usage																				
13. Relative Clause	3	1		*4*	1															
14. Ad Hoc								1 *1*			1	*1*								
Total:	**18**	**8**	**13**	**6** *45*	**4**	**4**	**8**	**6** *22*	**11**	**1**	**17**	*29*	**5**	**3**	**9**	*17*	**7**	**6**	**25**	**1** *39*

*Modal Type: S = Subjunctive; M = Modal Auxiliary Construction; P = Modal Preterite Inflection; N = Non-Distinctive Subjunctive.

Table 9: (continued)

Number of Text:	11				12				13				14				15			
Modal Type*:	S	M	P	N	S	M	P	N	S	M	P	N	S	M	P	N	S	M	P	N
Category:																				
1. Wish-Curse	1			*5*					1				9	10	*6*		1	1	1	*3*
2. Command														2		*2*				*7*
3. Indirect Narrative																				
4. Noun Clause 1	2				2	1	1	2			1	*1*	2	1		*3*	2	5		*7*
5. Noun Clause 2																				
6. Purpose										2		*2*		2			1	1		*3*
7. Result										2	1	*1*						1	1	*1*
8. Comparison								*1*												
9. Concession	1	1	1	*3*			1		2			*2*	2	1		*1*			1	
10. Time																		1	3	
11. Conditional	4	2	3	*9*	1	5		*6*	6	1	4	*6*	11	1	1	*6*	8	10	5	*15*
12. Polite Usage																				
13. Relative Clause																				
14. Ad Hoc																	2			*2*
Total:	7	3	4	5	*19*	1	2	8	*11*	4	7	7	9	*27*	8	5	7	*20*	14	7	13	1	*35*

*Modal Type: S = Subjunctive; M = Modal Auxiliary Construction; P = Modal Preterite Inflection; N = Non-Distinctive Subjunctive.

Table 9: (continued)

Number of Text:	16					17					18					19					20				
Modal Type*:	S	M	P	N		S	M	P	N		S	M	P	N		S	M	P	N		S	M	P	N	
Category:																									
1. Wish-Curse	4			7	*11*			1		*1*	5	1	1		*7*						3				*3*
2. Command		1			*1*			2		*2*		1			*1*							2			*2*
3. Indirect Narrative																									
4. Noun Clause 1	1	2	1		*4*			2		*2*		1			*1*			1		*1*					
5. Noun Clause 2				1	*1*				1	*1*															
6. Purpose	1				*1*									1	*1*										
7. Result																									
8. Comparison						1	2			*3*				1	*1*										
9. Concession																									
10. Time																									
11. Conditional	5	1	5		*11*			5		*5*								9		*9*	1		7		*8*
12. Polite Usage				1	*1*			3		*3*															
13. Relative Clause																									
14. Ad Hoc																									
Total:	11	4	6	9	*30*	1	2	13	1	*17*	5	3	1	2	*11*			10		*10*	4	2	7		*13*

*Modal Type: S = Subjunctive; M = Modal Auxiliary Construction; P = Modal Preterite Inflection; N = Non-Distinctive Subjunctive.

Table 10: Relative Percentages of Modal Forms in Dramatic Texts

Percentages of Subjunctive Modal Forms According to Type

*Number of Text:	1	2	3	4	5	6	7	8	9	10
Subjunctive Modal Auxiliary Construction	54.5	54.5	69.7	81.0	60.5	46.1	25.0	37.9	29.4	18.4
Modal Preterite Inflection	39.4	24.2	9.0	10.8	2.6	20.5	25.0	3.4	17.6	15.8
	6.0	21.2	21.2	8.1	36.8	33.3	50.0	58.6	52.9	65.7

Percentages of Non-Distinctive Modal Forms Per Total Subjunctive Modal Structures

Number of Text:	1	2	3	4	5	6	7	8	9	10
	19.5	37.7	0	5.1	5.0	13.3	37.5	0	0	2.5

Percentages of Inflected Subjunctives and of Total Subjunctive Modal Structures Per Total Finite Verbs

Number of Text:	1	2	3	4	5	6	7	8	9	10
Subjunctive	5.0	3.6	4.6	6.0	4.6	3.6	0.8	2.2	1.0	1.4
Subjunctive Modal Structure	9.1	6.6	6.6	7.4	7.6	7.8	3.2	5.8	3.4	7.6

Table 10: (continued)

Percentages of Subjunctive Modal Forms According to Type

*Number of Text:	11	12	13	14	15	16	17	18	19	20
Subjunctive	50.0	9.1	22.2	40.0	41.1	52.4	6.2	55.5	0	30.7
Modal Auxiliary Construction	21.4	18.2	38.8	25.0	20.5	19.0	12.5	33.3	0	15.4
Modal Preterite Inflection	28.5	72.7	38.8	35.0	38.2	28.6	81.2	11.1	100	53.8

Percentages of Non-Distinctive Modal Forms Per Total Subjunctive Modal Structures

Number of Text:	11	12	13	14	15	16	17	18	19	20
	26.3	0	33.3	0	2.8	30.0	5.9	18.1	0	0

Percentages of Inflected Subjunctives and of Total Subjunctive Modal Structures Per Total Finite Verbs

Number of Text:	11	12	13	14	15	16	17	18	19	20
Subjunctive	1.4	0.2	0.8	1.6	2.8	2.2	0.2	1.0	0	0.8
Subjunctive Modal Structure	2.8	2.2	3.6	4.0	6.8	4.2	3.2	1.8	2.0	2.6

Table 11: Type and Category of Subjunctive Modal Structures in Dramatic Texts

Number of Text*:	15a					16a					19a					20a				
Modal Type**:	S	M	P	N	*N*	S	M	P	N	*N*	S	M	P	N	*N*	S	M	P	N	*N*
Category:																				
1. Wish																1			1	*1*
2. Command	2	1						2		*2*						1				*1*
3. Indirect Narrative								1						1	*1*					
4. Noun Clause 1	1	2			*3*		1	2					2		*2*			5		*5*
5. Noun Clause 2																				
6. Purpose																				
7. Result																				
8. Comparison	2	1	1		*4*		2			*3*				1				1		*1*
9. Concession														1						
10. Time																				
11. Conditional	1	2	7		*10*		11	1	12			3			*3*		5			*5*
12. Polite Usage			2		*2*		4		4			8			*8*		4			*4*
13. Relative Clause			3		*3*												1			*1*
14. Ad Hoc			1		*1*								3		*3*					
Total:	6	6	16	5	*33*	1		20	3	*24*	1	1	16		*18*		1	16	1	*18*

Relative Percentages of Modal Forms in Dramatic Texts. Percentages of Modal Forms According to Type

Number of Text*:	15a	16a	19a	20a
Subjunctive	21.4	4.7	5.6	0
Modal Auxiliary Construction	21.4	0	5.6	5.9
Modal Preterite Inflection	57.2	95.3	88.8	94.1

Percentages of Non-Distinctive Modal Forms per Total Subjunctive Modal Structures

Number of Text*:	15a	16a	19a	20a
	15.1	12.5	0	5.6

Percentages of Inflected Subjunctives and of Subjunctive Modal Structures per Total Finite Verb Constructions

Number of Text*:	15a	16a	19a	20a
Subjunctive	1.2	0.2	0.2	0
Subjunctive Modal Structure	5.6	4.2	3.6	3.4

*See pages 82–83 for numbering of dramatic texts
**Modal Type: S = Subjunctive; M = Modal Auxiliary Construction; P = Modal Preterite Inflection; N = Non-Distinctive Subjunctive.

Index